W9-APM-346

LIFE
The Year in Pictures
2002

9/11/02 in NYC

At 6:40 a.m., on the anniversary of September 11, Arlene Pacheco and Michael Johnson make their way to work in Manhattan aboard the Staten Island Ferry. This picture is one of many taken throughout the city that day by an army of photographers from the renowned Eddie Adams Workshop. An exclusive sample from the project begins on page 84.

Photograph by Danielle Austen

LIFE
The Year in Pictures

The Games Begin

Five months after the horrific attacks on the United States, citizens of the world came to America and rededicated themselves to peaceful pursuits at the Opening Ceremonies of the 2002 Salt Lake City Winter Olympics.

Photograph by Mitchell Layton/Newsport

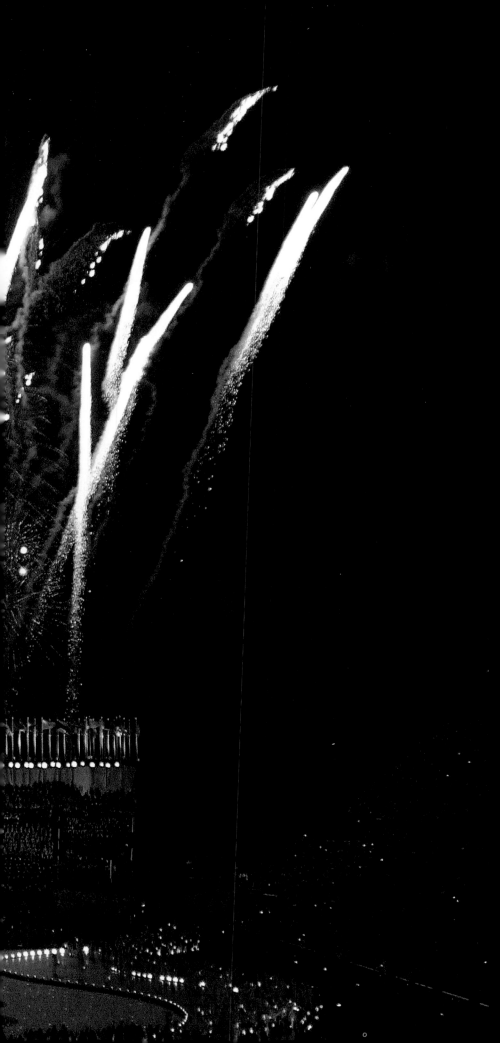

LIFE

Editor Robert Sullivan
Creative Director Ian Denning
Picture Editor Barbara Baker Burrows
Executive Editor Robert Andreas
Associate Picture Editors Christina Lieberman, Vivette Porges
Senior Reporter Hildegard Anderson
Writer/Reporter Lauren Nathan
Copy J.C. Choi (Chief), Bruce Diamond
Production Manager Michael Roseman
Picture Research Lauren Steel
Photo Assistant Joshua Colow
Consulting Picture Editor (London) Suzanne Hodgart

Publisher Andrew Blau
Director of Business Development Marta Bialek
Finance Director Camille Sanabria
Assistant Finance Manager Karen Tortora

Editorial Operations Richard K. Prue (Director),
Richard Shaffer (Manager), Brian Fellows, Raphael Joa,
Stanley E. Moyse (Supervisors), Keith Aurelio, Gregg Baker,
Charlotte Coco, Scott Dvorin, Kevin Hart, Rosalie Khan,
Po Fung Ng, Barry Pribula, David Spatz, Vaune Trachtman,
Sara Wasilausky, David Weiner

Time Inc. Home Entertainment

President Rob Gursha
Vice President, Branded Businesses David Arfine
Executive Director, Marketing Services Carol Pittard
Director, Retail & Special Sales Tom Mifsud
Director of Finance Tricia Griffin
Marketing Director Kenneth Maehlum
Assistant Marketing Director Ann Marie Doherty
Prepress Manager Emily Rabin
Book Production Manager Jonathan Polsky
Associate Product Manager Jennifer Dowell

Special thanks to Suzanne DeBenedetto, Robert Dente,
Gina Di Meglio, Anne-Michelle Gallero, Peter Harper, Robert
Marasco, Natalie McCrea, Jessica McGrath, Mary Jane Rigoroso,
Steven Sandonato, Bozena Szwagulinski, Niki Whelan

Published by

LIFE Books

Time Inc.
1271 Avenue of the Americas,
New York, NY 10020

Copyright 2003 Time Inc.
All rights reserved. No part
of this publication may be
reproduced in any form or by
any electronic or mechanical
means, including information
storage and retrieval systems,
without permission in writing
from the publisher, except
by a reviewer, who may quote
brief passages in a review.

ISBN: 1-929049-91-9
ISSN: 1092-0463

"LIFE" is a trademark of
Time Inc.

We welcome your comments
and suggestions about LIFE
Books. Please write to us at:
LIFE Books,
Attention: Book Editors,
PO Box 11016,
Des Moines, IA 50336-1016

If you would like to order any
of our hardcover Collector's
Edition books, please call us
at 1-800-327-6388 (Monday
through Friday, 7:00 a.m.–
8:00 p.m. or Saturday, 7:00
a.m.–6:00 p.m. Central Time).

Please visit us, and sample
past editions of LIFE, at
www.LIFE.com.

Iconic images from the LIFE Picture Collection are now available
as fine art prints and posters. The prints are reproductions on
archival, resin-coated photographic paper, framed in black
wood, with an acid-free mat. Works by the famous LIFE
photographers—Eisenstaedt, Parks, Bourke-White, Burrows,
among many others—are available. The LIFE poster collection
presents large-format, affordable, suitable-for-framing images.
For more information on the prints, priced at $99 each, call
888-933-8873 or go to www.purchaseprints.com. The posters
may be viewed and ordered at www.LIFEposters.com.

Darkness and Light

Whatever days, weeks and months came in the wake of September 11 were bound to be different as well as difficult. The year 2002 fit both descriptions, but it was also a time of recovery, pride and even uplift.

Hussein brandishes a sword given to him for his 65th birthday. On September 11, visitors to the Empire State Building ponder a diminished skyline.

Shadows. A reporter for *The Wall Street Journal* sets out for a meeting only to disappear into the shadows of a Pakistan rent by deadly internecine strife. Revelations show that, for decades, Catholic priests sexually abused countless young people, with the clerics' abominable behavior kept under wraps by superiors. Disclosures in other arenas indicate that, for years, corporate high rollers have also been hiding their own immoral and seemingly illegal behavior. Osama bin Laden continues to move in the shadows, stepping forth late in the year to taunt the free world from behind a tape-recorded message. Suicide bombers walk into clubs and cafes, sacrificing their crucial anonymity only at the last, murderous second. Children vanish, taken from their homes by . . . by whom? A neighbor? A presumed friend? A sniper is on the loose, hiding somewhere in the shadows, taking confident aim, dispensing death.

Two shadows loomed larger than all others: that of September 11 and that of Iraq. The former was about aftershock, fallout and recovery, and it stubbornly permeated life in the United States from January through December. The latter was all about what lay ahead. Would Saddam Hussein allow U.N. weapons inspectors in, and would their work be sufficiently unfettered to satisfy the U.S. that an Iraqi threat could be defused without war? All year the question played out, while the hum of tension in the world was interrupted at regular intervals by another terrorist explosion, another security alert, another arrest of another operative with "links to al-Qaeda"—yet another cause for fear and alarm.

Chris Trotman/Duomo

glamour event with a performance of pure joy, we found ourselves transported. Other stories, too, had a similar antidotal effect. When it appeared that the trapped Pennsylvania miners might be another sorrowful chapter in a year of woe, all nine men emerged alive, lifting spirits everywhere. A dogged adventurer from Chicago claimed his grail by finally circumnavigating the globe solo in a balloon, proving that if at first you don't succeed you should try, try, try—and try—again. Even some of the saddest stories came with gleaming silver linings. On October 15 a gift of $1,414, 356.46 was sent to the city of New York, per a stipulation in the will of the late Joe Temeczko, a Polish immigrant who had been a prisoner of war during World War II. No one knows how Joe, who died at the age of 86, saved that much money during his life as a self-employed handyman, or what compelled him to donate the whole of his fortune to New York City, but these things he did—making the bequest in memory of the victims of 9/11.

This was going to be, one way or another, the year that immediately followed and was constantly affected by that awful day, September 11. The year 2002 proved to be an extraordinary time of trial and triumph, recovery and resolve: a year of shadow and occasional, brilliant light.

In the face of so much fretfulness, the human spirit once again showed a remarkable resilience and an unquenchable capacity for optimism. As one example: the Olympics. Never before had this extravaganza been so set up for failure, what with a pre-Games bribery scandal and, then, the thought that post-9/11 security would stifle, sucking all fun out of the pageant. The bizarre French-Russian vote-swapping affair among figure skating judges didn't help much, either. But as young snowboarders swooped and swooshed, as Canadian hockey players swept toward the goal and, finally, as Long Island teenager Sarah Hughes won the Olympics'

Hughes captures the hearts of her fellow Americans with a bravura performance. In death, Temeczko captures their imaginations with an act of uncommon generosity.

relief. Early on, in an upset for the ages, a football team from New England—named the Patriots, and what could be more apt?—won the Super Bowl. Then, a short time later, the United States hosted a marvelous Winter Olympics in and around Salt Lake City. Ultratight security and a judging scandal in pairs figure skating could not overshadow a joyous display of energy, athleticism and brotherhood. Right: 1992 Olympic gold medalist Kristi Yamaguchi of the U.S. dazzles during the opening ceremonies. Two weeks later, another American was crowned Skating Queen: 16-year-old Sarah Hughes of Long Island.

Photograph by Kenneth Jarecke/Contact

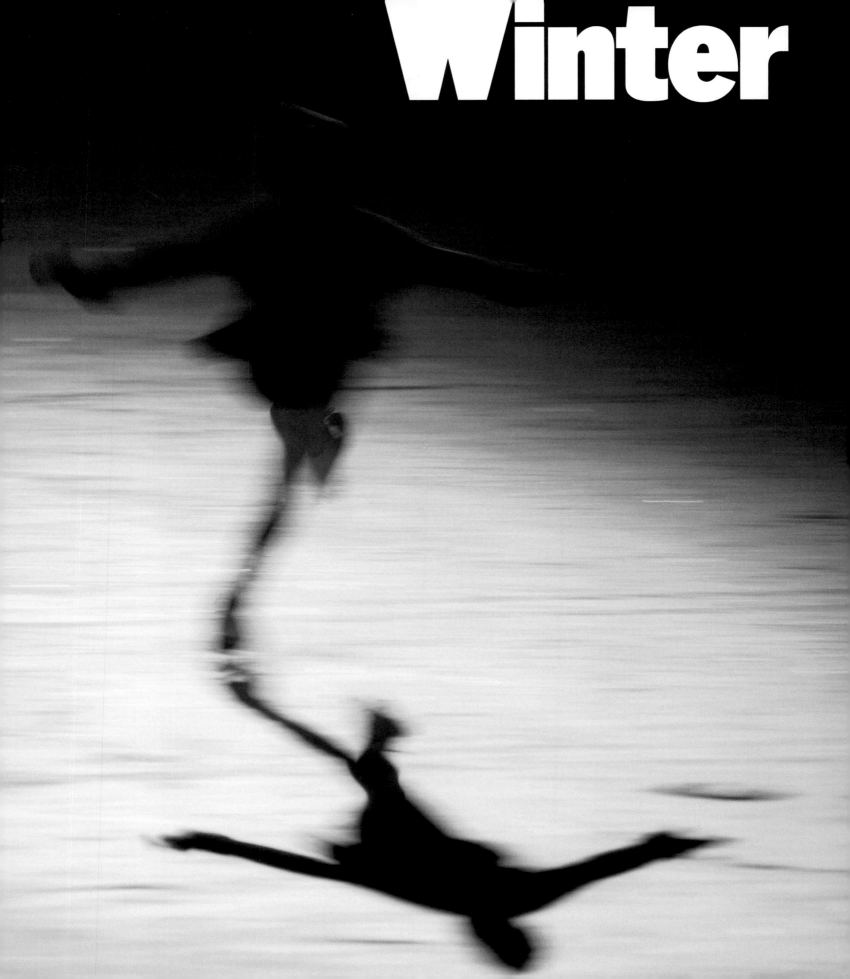

Winter

Now She Has a Name

She had been known for 17 years, ever since Steve McCurry's remarkable portrait graced the cover of *National Geographic* magazine, as "the Afghan girl." In January, in the wake of Afghanistan's liberation, McCurry returned to the tormented land along with a team from National Geographic Television and Film's *Explorer* series to search for her. He showed the picture around Nasir Bagh, the refugee camp where he had encountered her long ago. A man knew her, and brought her from the mountains near Tora Bora to the camp. She has a family now, but life, of course, has been hard. She had her picture taken for the second time in 17 years. Her name, we now know, is Sharbat Gula.

Photographs by Steve McCurry Magnum

❝ Afghanistan has been in a Dark Age for two decades. That she's resurfaced now is perhaps prophetic, a hopeful sign. We'll have to wait and see. ❞

—**Steve McCurry,** photographer

Jan. 1 In Times Square, moments into the New Year, a tearful Michael Bloomberg is sworn in as **New York City's 108th mayor** by his predecessor, Rudolph Giuliani, 111 days after September 11.

Jan. 5 Troubled 15-year-old Charles Bishop steals a single-engine plane and **crashes into a Tampa skyscraper.** His suicidal flight initially provokes fears of terrorism.

Jan. 7 British Prime Minister Tony Blair, the **first world leader to visit Afghanistan** since the fall of the Taliban, meets with his counterpart, Hamid Karzai, and pledges support for the country's new leaders.

Anguished Liberty

An earlier replica of the Statue of Liberty in China represented a show of defiance in 1989 when students demonstrating in Beijing's Tiananmen Square took America's great symbol as their own. The Communist government, of course, quashed that revolt. There was no controversy in January 2002, however, when a sculpture at the International Snow and Ice Festival in the northern city of Harbin looked to the horror of September 11. In a year that saw rising anti-Americanism from nations objecting to the U.S. campaign in Afghanistan, its involvement in the Middle East and its stance toward Iraq, the freely expressed sympathy in China, ardent foe of democracy, was welcome.

Photograph China Photo/Reuters/Landov

Jan. 24 Workers begin to dismantle a **200-foot Ferris wheel** in Paris after a judge orders its removal. Built for the millennium celebration, many consider it an eyesore. The wheel's owner says, "They're tossing us out like Kleenex."

Jan. 29 In his first State of the Union address, President George W. Bush focuses on **national and homeland security,** vowing to win the war against terrorism while "embracing a new ethic and a new creed: 'Let's roll.'"

Feb. 2 Seven-year-old Danielle van Dam disappears from her suburban San Diego bedroom. After 25 days her body is found, and samples of hair, fibers and fingerprints match those found in the home of neighbor David Westerfield, later convicted of her murder. A number of **kidnappings** make headlines during the year.

Feb. 3 Red, white and blue confetti blankets the New Orleans Superdome after Cinderella quarterback Tom Brady and the New England Patriots stun the St. Louis Rams, 20–17, in **Super Bowl XXXVI.**

Rage at the Ice Rink

It has long been axiomatic that athletics can play an important role in molding the young. The lessons taken from victory and defeat, it is thought, help prepare one for the ups and downs of life. But organized leagues have become the way kids play most team sports, and an ugly problem has developed in recent years wherein out-of-control parents end up humiliating themselves, their kids and their communities. Or worse. At left, Thomas Junta reenacts a fight in which he killed another hockey dad, Michael Costin, during their sons' practice in Reading, Mass. On January 25, Junta was sentenced to six to 10 years for involuntary manslaughter.

Photograph by Steve Senne
Reuters/Landov

" Three of Mr. Costin's four children saw their father get beaten to death. "

—**Judge Charles M. Grabau**

Feb. 6 Four million chocolate Easter bunnies melt when a fire destroys a warehouse in Volketswil, Switzerland.

Feb. 7 Residents of Bogotá, Colombia, hike, bike or skate in **a one-day ban on autos.** A businessman riding a two-seater with his wife through the city of seven million calls it "a good opportunity to take away stress and lower air pollution."

Feb. 12 At the National Sea Life Center in Birmingham, England, loudspeakers croon **Barry White love songs** to five male and five female sharks—all celibate—in the hope that the music will "tempt them into feeling more romantic."

Feb. 13 Queen Elizabeth II bestows an honorary knighthood on former New York City Mayor Rudolph Giuliani. Because he is not British, he is **not dubbed Sir Rudy.**

Images Sans Frontieres

What Makes a POW?

By February, 158 prisoners taken in Afghanistan were jailed at the U.S. Navy base at Guantánamo Bay, Cuba (left). When photos of the shackled, blindfolded men circulated, charges of brutality were heard. The U.S., while insisting there was no mistreatment, said the detainees, who finally numbered more than 600 from some 44 countries, were illegal combatants not entitled to Geneva Convention protections. Still, in November, the Pentagon went ballistic when photos of tethered prisoners apparently being transported from the battleground were leaked.

Photograph by Shane T. McCoy
Reuters/Landov

Feb. 15 A dog-walker in Walker County, Ga., comes upon a skull, leading to the **grisly discovery** of scores of bodies in unmarked graves. Instead of being cremated they have been "stacked like cordwood" or strewn about the backyard by the owners of the Tri-State Crematory. Evidence suggests that the company's furnace hasn't worked for years.

First in a Series

The business of America may or may not be business, but without question, the members of our society rely on money to provide the basic needs of life. And most are willing to do an honest day's work to get that money. So while no one expects the real world to provide a level playing field, there is an assumption that, robber barons notwithstanding, our business leaders should play fair when it comes to people's life savings. Some of the folks at Enron apparently thought otherwise as they wolfed down huge profits while leaving the average Joe with diddly to retire on. (Here: Chairman Kenneth Lay, who took solace in the Fifth Amendment, and whistle-blower Sherron Watkins, who said in November she would leave the firm.) Throughout the year, with one greedy company after another, the list of infamy grew, but for those employees whose futures had been sabotaged, the prospect of jail for the bossmen was slight balm.

Photograph Gamma
Photograph by Stephen J. Boitano Gamma

" I am incredibly nervous that we will implode in a wave of accounting scandals. "

—**Watkins,** in a 2001 memo to Lay, made public by Congress on January 14, 2002

Feb. 26 A Kansas City, Mo., pharmacist pleads guilty to **tampering with chemotherapy drugs,** thereby endangering 34 cancer patients. In the first of more than 400 lawsuits brought against millionaire Robert R. Courtney, a jury awards $2.2 billion in October to plaintiff Georgia Hayes.

Feb. 27 At the 44th Grammys, top honors go to U2 for "Walk On" (single), Alicia Keys for "Fallin'" (song), and various artists for "O Brother, Where Art Thou?" (album). **The talented Keys** wins four other awards.

Jacky Naegelen/Reuters

Trouble on Main Street

Natural disasters assume many forms, but there is something particularly primitive, something especially ghastly, about a volcano and its unstoppable lava flow. In mid-January, the 400,000 residents of the Congo port city of Goma fled desperately when molten magma as deep as six feet left 147 dead and the city, in the words of a rescue worker, "flat, black and burning." Refugees received care in hastily set up hospices (above, in neighboring Rwanda). Said one young man, whose workplace and home were both destroyed, "People have been through a lot—war, violence, poverty—now we must face the volcano."

Photograph by George Mulala

Reuters/Landov

March 1 NASA's Odyssey spacecraft finds yet more evidence of water on Mars. Further proof of **life on the Red Planet?**

March 2 Operation Anaconda begins with U.S. B-52 strikes on suspected Taliban and al-Qaeda quarters in Afghanistan. **Hundreds of enemy fighters** are killed by American and allied forces during the assault, the largest of the war.

In the Holy Land

It was a brutal year in the Middle East as Palestinians and Israelis engaged in a fatal cycle of attack and reprisal. The hallmark of the Palestinian offensive was suicide bombing, with martyrs to the cause killing scores of civilians in cafes and on buses. The Israeli Army responded with might. Tanks laid siege to Yasir Arafat's compound and rolled through other Arab enclaves, accompanied by soldiers searching house to house for militants. On March 7, in the West Bank town of Tulkarem, a woman stands by as a commando comes through the window. Later, loudspeakers demand that all males between the ages of 15 and 45 report for interrogation.

Photograph by David Silverman Getty

❝ My vision is two states, living side by side, in peace and security . . . For the sake of humanity, things must change in the Middle East. ❞

— U.S. President George W. Bush

March 7 Johns Hopkins astronomers announce that **the universe** is sort of beige-colored. Two months earlier they had concluded that it was turquoise.

March 8 In Jaipur, India, 81 bookies are arrested for offering odds on whether **religious riots** would break out in a nearby state where hundreds of lives had been lost to violence. Panic strikes Jaipur after the bookies, trying to drum up business, start rumors of impending riots.

March 10 With the **Middle East in flames,** the Bush administration sends Vice President Dick Cheney to the region as part of a 12-country mission that will focus on U.S. intentions toward Iraq and on winning support for the war on terror.

"Tunnel of Death"

A train bound from Cairo for Luxor erupted in flames on February 20, killing 361 passengers in the worst rail tragedy in Egyptian history. Most of the dead were poor folks heading for a Muslim holy festival. A portable gas stove, commonly used to brew tea and coffee in third class, started the blaze, which burned as the train sped full-throttle for 15 minutes before halting. Lights in the cars went out as horrified riders tried to fight their way through window bars designed to keep people from getting a free ride. Mothers threw children through the bars trying to save them. Said one survivor, "It was hell."

Photograph by Aladin Abdel Naby
Reuters/Landov

March 12 Homeland Security chief Tom Ridge outlines a **five-color warning system** for ranking terrorist alerts: from green (lowest risk), to blue, yellow, orange and red (the highest danger level).

March 12 After a monthlong trial, a Houston jury convicts 37-year-old Andrea Yates of murder. Rejecting her insanity defense, they send her to a minimum of 40 years in prison. Yates admitted that she had **drowned her five children.**

March 24 The 74th Academy Awards show sounds a historic note as Halle Berry becomes **the first African American** to win Best Actress, Denzel Washington the second to take home Best Actor, and veteran Sidney Poitier is given an honorary Oscar. *A Beautiful Mind* is recognized as the Best Picture, but the buzz afterward centers on the memorable speeches from the three black performers.

A Fitting Tribute

The notion that a phantom image of the Twin Towers might be a suitable memorial to the victims of September 11 occurred almost simultaneously to the heads of a firm specializing in architectural computer modeling, to an architect, and to two artists who had worked out of an office on the 91st floor of one of the towers. The five men, joined by an architectural lighting expert and supported by two cooperating nonprofit arts groups, created a beautiful thing. For 32 nights starting on the six-month anniversary of the attacks, "Tribute in Light," composed of two parallel beams formed by eighty-eight 7,000-watt searchlights projected a mile into the sky, spurred reflection and remembrance. Here, the path of an airplane creates a poignant, if chilling, effect.

Photograph by Tomas Muscionico Contact

❝ It's like a votive candle. It will have its time and its place. And then, it will go out. ❞

—**Saskia Levy,** project organizer for the Municipal Art Society

March 25 An **earthquake** measuring 6.0 strikes northern Afghanistan. It is believed that some 800 people perish in the second such disaster within a month.

March 27 Police in Slidell, La., pursue a 15-mile-long **trail of doughnuts** en route to nabbing two thieves who have made off with an unattended Krispy Kreme truck.

March 29 After an increasing number of victims fall to suicide bombers, Israeli tanks and bulldozers attack the Ramallah compound where **Palestinian leader Yasir Arafat** is trapped. Israeli Prime Minister Ariel Sharon labels the strife "a long and complicated war that knows no borders."

Shannon Stapleton

Vincenzo Pinto/Reuters/Landow

FOCUS ON | Scandal in the Church

Pain. Rage. Hatred. But of all the emotions elicited by the news that, for decades, Roman Catholic priests throughout America—and the world—had been sexually abusing the young while being shielded by their superiors, the most prevalent was a piercing feeling of betrayal.

It Was More Than Just Boston

It was Australia, Ireland and the pope's homeland, Poland. In the U.S., the scandal knew no bounds: Clergy from California to Connecticut, Maine to Florida were suspended, put on trial or put in jail. Pope John Paul II finally summoned his American cardinals to Rome. On April 22, Boston Archbishop Bernard Law—himself accused of a cover-up during a winter of testimony in the trial of a predator priest—and fellow chastened prelates arrived at a Vatican shrouded in clouds (opposite). Later, back in the U.S., bishops drafted a "zero tolerance" policy on abusers, but it was subsequently vetoed by the Vatican. In November, a revised plan, which would establish tribunals to investigate each case, was sent to Rome.

George Martell/Boston Herald

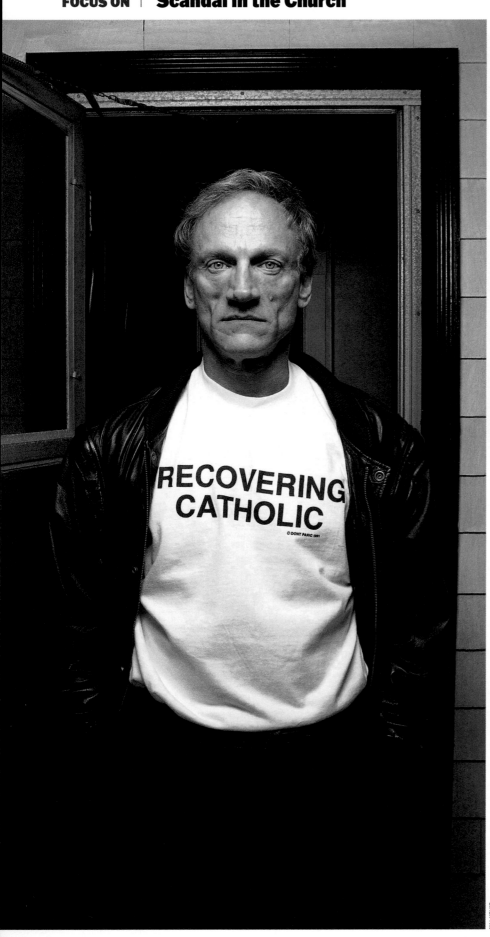

Ethan Hill

A Catholic Bastion Under Siege

Yes, it was more than Boston. But it was the disclosures there that turned the Church scandal into a ferocious controversy. Revelations during the trial of Rev. John Geoghan (above), plus those in *The Boston Globe,* shocked Catholics, and others, from coast to coast. In January the *Globe* reported that the Boston archdiocese had continually reassigned Geoghan, whom it knew to be a child molester, for three decades, putting ever more boys in harm's way. In February, Geoghan, 66, was sentenced to nine to 10 years in jail for indecently assaulting a 10-year-old, but plaintiffs' lawyers in civil suits said his victims might number more than 130. The call for Cardinal Law's head was general, sounded loudest by such as Phil Saviano (left), founder of a Survivors Network chapter. Saviano, who claimed he had been molested decades ago by Rev. David Holley, a Massachusetts priest who in 1993 was sentenced to 275 years for child abuse, said the Church was turning its back on victims to protect its own. Law (opposite) shifted policy, approving settlements in hopes of ending the Geoghan matter and giving authorities the names of scores of priests accused of abuse.

Jim Bourg/Reuters/Landov

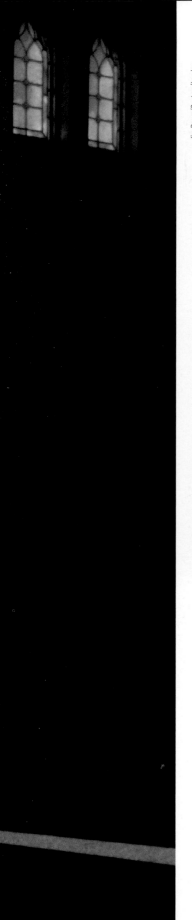

No Sanctuary, No Amen

The year was long and sad in Boston. Left: In March, while the cardinal is saying Mass at the Cathedral of the Holy Cross, a deacon peers out at protesters praying for abuse victims. Above: In May, Law, during a break in his legal deposition in a civil suit, gives Holy Communion at Our Lady of Perpetual Help Mission Church in Boston's Roxbury section. Right: By summer, Voice of the Faithful, a lay organization led by James Muller, calls for reform and archdiocesan accountability. Law disregarded the group's recommendations, but his troubles wouldn't go away. In June, Rev. Paul Shanley, who was allegedly Geoghan's match as a predator and who had been arrested in California and brought back to Massachusetts, pleaded not guilty to 10 counts of child rape and six of indecent assault and battery. Documents in the case, released in December, described ever more ghastly behavior in the archdiocese, and Law finally had to step down.

| # Daniel Pearl

His murder became a chapter in the September 11 saga and made him an international symbol. Behind the headlines and the horror was a gentle man, valued friend, talented reporter, loving husband, father-to-be. A guy named Danny.

Birmingham High School/AP

In 1981 bright young Danny (middle row, head on hand) took part in the Knowledge Bowl during his senior year at Birmingham High in Van Nuys. He had an active mind and remained open to everything. "People who we believed were the epitome of boredom, he found to be interesting, even intriguing," said his father. "Little did we know that talking to strangers would one day invite this tragedy."

Come out, come out, the world is not such a bad place./Come out, come out, there's someone smiling upon you." This song lyric by a gone and forgotten 1990s band called Clamp expresses well the infectious positivism of the group's fiddler, Danny (never Dan) Pearl. It was beyond his ken that this wonderful world, Pearl's oyster for 38 years, would turn vicious, then fatal, in the dark days of a brutal Pakistani winter.

He was never not sunny, according to those who knew him best. Born in Princeton, N.J., to Israeli parents, he grew up happy-go-lucky in the Los Angeles suburb of Encino. He was blessed with a "unique biological phenomenon," said his father, Judea, at a private memorial service for Danny in

March. "There was no malice in his body. Not one little shred. You try to bully him, he didn't cry. He didn't bully back. He'd just look at you in the eye and wait for you to realize how silly you would look when it's all over." At the same service, Daniel Gill remembered his best friend as "the great big kid, the goofball, the king of clutter, the loser of tickets."

If Danny was notorious throughout his life for a lack of organizational skills—he was known to search frantically for keys that had been left in the lock—he was nonetheless smart and talented. Neither a nerd nor a slacker, he loved playing violin in the local youth orchestra or reenacting favorite Monty Python skits with Gill and their pal Craig Sherman. His brains were his ticket north to Stanford, where he let his hair and beard grow, and

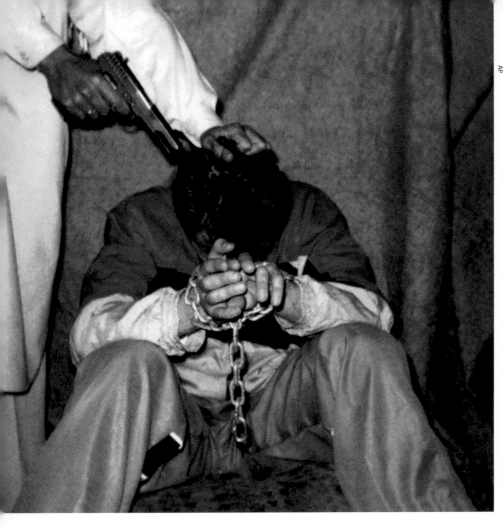

AP

On January 27, the media received images of Pearl shackled, along with the news that he was being held to protest treatment of Taliban and al-Qaeda prisoners. Weeks later, a video of Pearl being stabbed and beheaded was circulated. Four militants were arrested; Ahmed Omar Saeed Sheikh (below) was convicted in Pakistan as the mastermind and sentenced to death.

Zia Mazhar/AP

found his enthusiasms deepening. He spun everything from Haydn to heavy metal as a late-night deejay on KZSU, and founded the short-lived *Stanford Commentary,* a publication dedicated to airing a variety of viewpoints on issues of importance.

Danny did the travel-and-ski-bum thing after graduation, then moved to the Northeast and began building a career in journalism, first at three newspapers in western Massachusetts and then at *The Wall Street Journal.* The scores of features that he wrote for that paper over more than a decade reflected his serious, inquisitive, sensitive and humorous sides. He wrote deftly of the mindset of fundamentalist Muslims and, on one occasion, of a group of American Southerners who were taking "accent reduction" lessons in an attempt to lose their drawl. An editor who admired Pearl, Lawrence Ingrassia, remembered that "Danny got noticed, right away, after starting at the *Journal* in 1990. For me, it wasn't for the beaming smile that the whole world now recognizes. It wasn't for his soft-spoken charm that lit up everything around him. It was for his generosity to friends, colleagues and strangers."

Danny, who made people share that smile, was a fellow who had little trouble getting dates. The love of his life turned out to be an exotic French-born broadcast journalist of Cuban and Dutch heritage whom he met at a party in Paris. Mariane and Danny wed at a French château in the summer of 1999, and looked to the future. "We're going to change the world," he told her.

Their path took them from Paris to Bombay, where Danny was assigned as the *Journal's* South Asia bureau chief. As war swept through Afghanistan in the aftermath of September 11, Pearl wrote dispatches both formal and informal, at one point E-mailing his parents, "Hi! It looks pretty dicey from here—at least your papers don't run front-page photos of the corpses of journalists."

In January, Danny Pearl was in Karachi, Pakistan, to report on the militant mentors of shoe-bomber Richard Reid. On the 23rd he went to a restaurant for an assignation with a prominent Muslim cleric. He never returned, and it is clear that he did not live long beyond his capture, that he was murdered in a most savage fashion.

Danny, said his father at the memorial service, always felt that "some good fairy would take care of him. And she did, for 38 years."

On May 28, Mariane gave birth to Adam Pearl in Paris. "Adam's birth rekindles the joy, love and humanity that Danny radiated wherever he went," Pearl's family said in a statement. "The name Adam symbolizes the birth of humankind and the connectedness of civilizations. Danny also liked the name Adam because it reminded him of President John Quincy Adams, whose ideas of freedom and peace were so far ahead of his time."

Cecile Gabriel

Hard Land, Hard Times

Just five years ago, these cattle in the Rio Grande Valley would have been underwater, but the drought that has racked much of the country certainly didn't spare Texas. Here, it's the end of June, and the preceding 12 months have been the driest ever in the Southwest. Conditions over a longer term were comparable to the worst episodes of the 20th century. By the end of July, more than a third of the Lower 48 was beset by severe drought. Agriculture and the cattle industry were hit hard, and water shortages were common. Not surprisingly, drought's sister calamity—fire—was flourishing.

Photograph by Jake Price/Sipa

Spring

A Church Under Siege

On April 2, in one of the more extraordinary events of Israel's tumultuous year, 30 Palestinian gunmen burst into Bethlehem's Church of the Nativity, believed by Christians to sit upon the site where Jesus was born. They were followed in by more than 200 Palestinian police and civilians. Israeli tanks approached but did not attack. For 39 days the standoff held: Christian clerics playing host to Palestinians, Israeli snipers keeping aim. A month into the stalemate, Carolyn Cole of the *Los Angeles Times* gained entrance to the church, then photographed the endgame. In a brokered settlement, 13 militants were exiled to Europe while 124 other Palestinians who had not already left the church were freed.

Photograph by Carolyn Cole
Los Angeles Times

❝ They pace together along the sanctuary floor, fingering their prayer beads, hoping for a way out. ❞

—**Carolyn Cole,** photographer

April 4 Nine photographers and a press motorcyclist are cleared of manslaughter charges in the death of Princess Diana and Dodi al-Fayed in Paris on Aug. 31, 1997. France's highest court upholds the dismissal despite claims by al-Fayed's father that **the pursuing press** forced the chauffeur, who also died, to drive faster.

April 5 Ace Japanese mountaineer Ken Noguchi and 28 others begin a **cleanup effort on Mount Everest.** With his third such venture, Noguchi hopes to bring back 3,300 pounds of garbage, along with frozen bodies that have been trapped under the ice. Some 180 climbers have died on the mountain.

All Systems Go

April 11, the Arabian Sea—In this photo taken from the aircraft carrier USS *John F. Kennedy,* a Navy F-14 Tomcat maneuvers in a hard, high G turn after releasing flares. These decoys may be manually or automatically dispensed by the fighter to divert heat-seeking missiles away from the engine. The "cloud" around the plane is condensed water vapor that results when humid air is subjected to pressure from the wings as they produce lift. The Tomcat is participating in a combat operation against al-Qaeda positions in Afghanistan.

Photograph by David Hume Kennerly

April 9 During a traffic check in Lewiston, Maine, a driver leaps from his car and heads for a nearby woods. Police in hot pursuit get some **"civilian" help** when a skunk suddenly sprays the suspect so enthusiastically that, for the moment, he couldn't have managed even a perp walk.

April 18 Three die and 29 are injured as a four-seater plane plows into Milan's Pirelli building, **the tallest skyscraper in Italy.** One onlooker expresses the response of many, that "it was like a movie, like what happened . . . in New York."

April 23 President Bush's close, longtime adviser Karen Hughes reveals that she and her family will **return to Texas.** "To be honest, I guess we're a little homesick."

April 25 Dentists arrive at the Shanghai Zoo to reattach 10-year-old Meina's tusk, broken when the elephant was being moved. With a pot of glue, the dental team restores the **titanic tooth.**

April 26 Erfurt, Germany, is the scene of a **deadly school massacre** as a recently expelled student moves from room to room with a rifle and a handgun, shooting 17 people and then himself.

A Monarch's Milestone

At an annual cost to the commoners of $50 million, and after years of silliness and scandal, the British monarchy was not at its popular high-water mark as it entered the new millennium. No matter: Throughout 2002, Britons largely put their qualms aside and huzzahed their queen on the 50th anniversary of her ascension to the throne. Elizabeth II's Jubilee prompted a four-day national holiday in June, capped by pomp and circumstance at Buckingham Palace, where Prime Minister Tony Blair addressed the queen: "You have adapted the monarchy successfully to the modern world and that has been a challenge because it is a world that can pay scant regard to tradition and often values passing fashions above enduring faith."

Photograph by Denis Waugh

❝ It has been a pretty remarkable 50 years by any standards. ❞

—**Queen Elizabeth II**

May 1 To commemorate the 1927 flight of Charles "Lucky" Lindbergh, his 36-year-old grandson, Erik, solos across the Atlantic in the ***New Spirit of St. Louis.*** He lands at Le Bourget Airport near Paris in about half the time it took Granddad.

May 4 War Emblem, **a 20-to-1 long shot,** wins the 128th running of the Kentucky Derby. The Thoroughbred also takes the Preakness, but an early stumble in the Belmont costs him the Triple Crown.

May 8 Luke Helder admits in federal court in Reno, Nev., that he placed 18 **pipe bombs in mailboxes** in five midwestern states, injuring six people and fanning terrorist fears across the nation. The 21-year-old student could face life in prison.

Smile, Little Sis

Minutes after losing to sister Serena in the finals of the French Open in June, Venus Williams joins the tennis paparazzi on center court to record the new champion's award ceremony. The 2002 season proved to be a transition in power, as Venus thrice yielded to her younger sibling in the finals of a major tournament: Serena topped Venus in straight sets at Wimbledon, then repeated the feat when she won her second U.S. Open. Serena wowed the crowd with her big game and with her body-clinging Lycra outfits. She also became one more example of the perils on the flashy women's tour: Even as she roared through the field at Flushing Meadows, a 34-year-old from Frankfurt, Germany, pleaded guilty in a crosstown Queens court to stalking Serena.

Photograph Angeli/ReflexNews

❝ I raised my game this year. I was just tired of losing. Life was passing me by. ❞

—**Serena Williams,** 21

May 10 Ex-FBI counterintelligence pro Robert Hanssen, 58, is sentenced to life without parole for handing documents to Moscow for cash and diamonds. Regarded as one of the **most damaging spies** in American history, Hanssen apologizes "for my behavior. I am ashamed by it."

May 13 President Bush says that the U.S. and Russia have agreed on a treaty "which will substantially **reduce our nuclear arsenals** to the agreed-upon range of 1,700 to 2,200 warheads . . . This treaty will liquidate the legacy of the cold war."

May 21 Merrill Lynch agrees to pay a **$100 million fine** for promoting stocks of companies that the firm wooed for its investment banking business.

Reuters

Preying on the Young

In a case that was a signal incident in a rash of child kidnappings, 14-year-old Elizabeth Smart was taken from her Salt Lake City home at gunpoint in the early hours of June 5. Her nine-year-old sister, Mary Catherine, said she saw a dark-haired man wearing a baseball cap who warned her to keep quiet. Searches in the hills around the Smart home by teams with dogs were unsuccessful. Eventually, attention began to focus on Richard Albert Ricci, a handyman who had done work for the Smarts and was being held on unrelated charges. He said he knew nothing and, in August, died after suffering a stroke—with Elizabeth Smart yet to be found.

Photograph by Steve C. Wilson AP

May 22 A **blistering heat wave** in southern India has killed more than a thousand people. Temperatures reach at least 122°, turning mud huts into furnaces.

May 22 The remains of 24-year-old **Chandra Levy** are found in a Washington, D.C., park. The former intern, linked romantically with California Congressman Gary Condit, was missing for 13 months.

A Spring Cold One

The 2002 summit of the G8, a group of the world's seven richest nations plus Russia, was held in June in Kananaskis, Alberta, in western Canada. The primary topics of discussion were terrorism, global economies and aid for Africa. Weighty subjects, to be sure, but as we know, all work and no play . . . Here, some of the planet's head honchos—from left, Canadian and British Prime Ministers Jean Chrétien and Tony Blair, an interpreter, President Bush and Italian PM Silvio Berlusconi—take a breather. Bush, for his part, savors a rare light moment in a tense year, along with a swig of nonalcoholic beer.

Photograph Sphinx/Timepix

June 7 Kennedy kin Michael C. Skakel is convicted of **killing his Greenwich, Conn., neighbor** Martha Moxley with a golf club in 1975, when both were 15 years old. Skakel is sentenced to 20 years to life.

June 10 Attorney General John Ashcroft announces the arrest of American citizen Abdullah al-Mujahir, 31, who, according to Ashcroft, had al-Qaeda links and plotted to build and explode a radioactive **"dirty bomb."** Born in Brooklyn as Jose Padilla, he converted to Islam and took on a new name. He was detained on May 8. Later, President Bush is said to have upbraided Ashcroft for inflating the case.

June 11 On a remote Irish estate, **Paul McCartney,** 59, weds model Heather Mills, 34. Ringo Starr, the other surviving Beatle, is among the 300 guests, who enjoy vegetarian Indian food on the castle lawn.

June 15 A Federal District Court jury in Houston finds Enron auditing firm Arthur Andersen guilty of obstructing justice by **destroying documents.** In July, Congress passes a bill imposing stiffer penalties for a variety of white-collar crimes.

The Beautiful Game

There have been many great soccer powers through the years: Argentina, Uruguay, Italy, West Germany. But no other country has ever contrived to blend style and power in such a superb, heady cocktail as that served by the boys of Brazil, who in June topped the Germans 2–0 in Yokohama to win their fifth World Cup. The brilliant 25-year-old striker Ronaldo, who had had a nightmare showing in the previous Cup final, netted both of the goals as his countrymen sambaed wildly in the stands. When the time comes for Earth to send a team to the Intergalactic Cup, rest assured that the rocket will depart from São Paulo.

Photograph by Catuffe Sipa

❝ We were feeling the positive energy of the support of the Brazilian people. ❞

—**Luiz Felipe Scolari,** Brazil's coach

June 16 Tiger Woods wins his eighth major, besting Phil Mickelson at the U.S. Open at Bethpage in Farmingdale, N.Y. The 26-year-old Woods led wire to wire.

June 18 A Palestinian **suicide bomber** kills 19 people and wounds at least 50 others on a rush-hour city bus in southern Jerusalem. Hamas, the Islamic militant group, claims responsibility for the slaughter.

June 19 The White House is evacuated when a single-engine Cessna **violates restricted airspace.** Two Air Force F-16s escort the plane to Richmond, where its pilot is released after questioning.

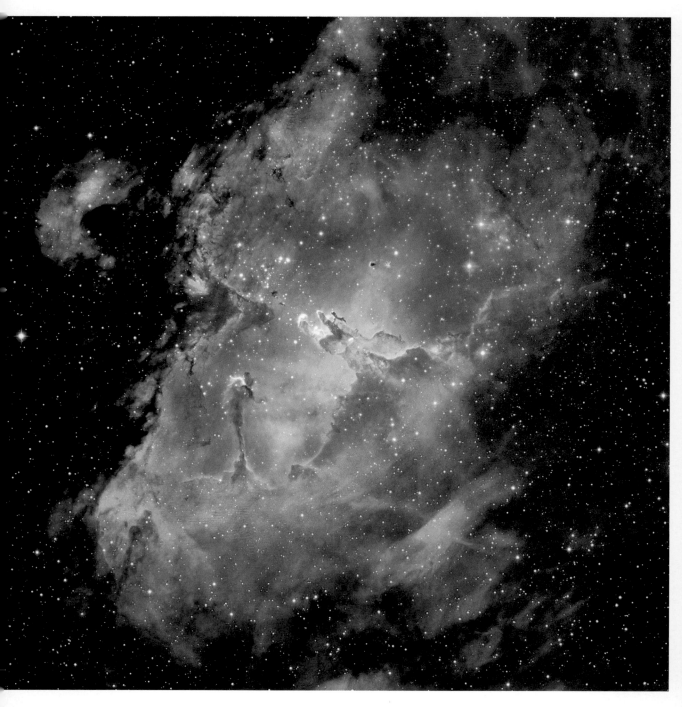

A Terrifying Grandeur

Year after year, the Hubble Space Telescope is making the world a smaller place. The frightening study in scarlet at right, taken in April by the new Advanced Camera for Surveys, shows about a third of the Cone Nebula, actually an innocuous amalgam of gas and dust whose entire length equals 64 million round-trips to the moon. In June, the Kitt Peak Observatory snapped the above panoramic image of the Pillars of Creation (at center), a famed Hubble subject that will, alas, fade away . . . in a million years.

Photographs by NASA

June 20 Astronomers reveal that an **asteroid the size of a football field** came within 75,000 miles of Earth on June 14. The near miss, one of the closest ever recorded, went undetected for three days. The space rock was going 23,000 mph.

June 24 Leading U.S. lawmakers cite evidence that al-Qaeda is regrouping. Alabama Senator Richard Shelby, the highest-ranking Republican on the Senate Intelligence Committee, states: **"They could hit us any day."**

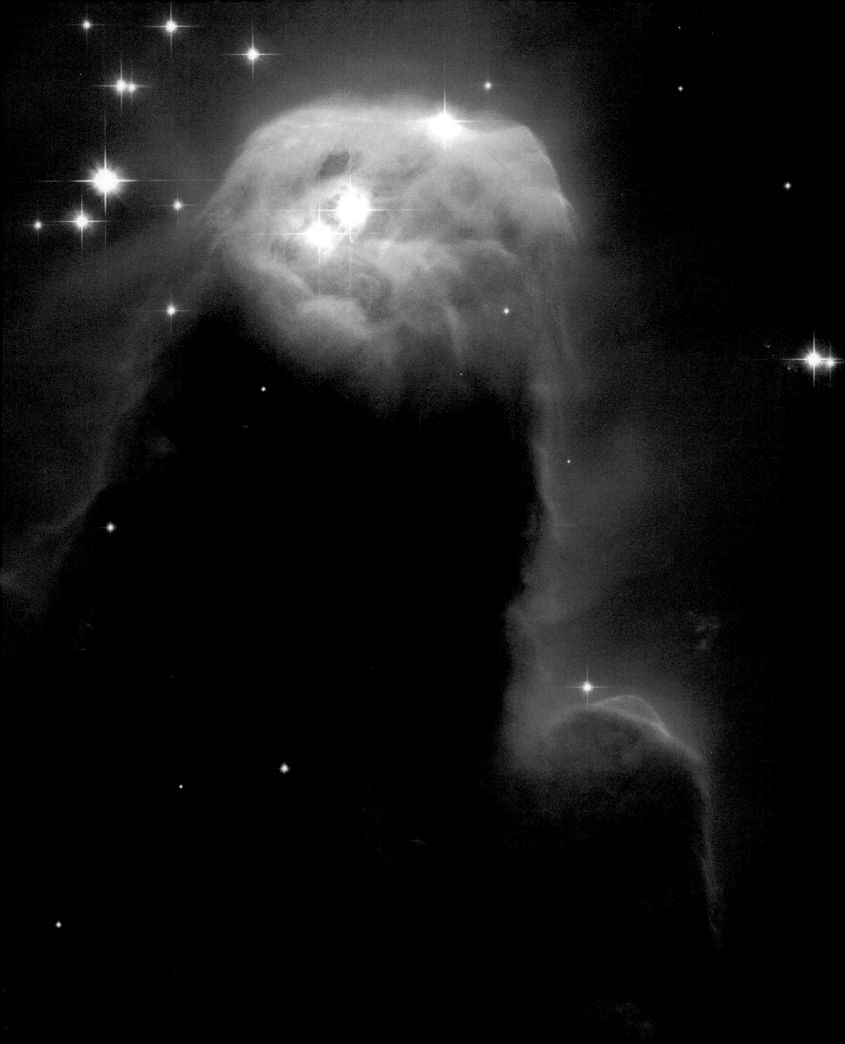

The largest wildfire in Arizona
history developed when two
blazes converged in June.
The Rodeo fire was allegedly
set by a seasonal firefighter
looking to get some work. The
Chediski fire was caused by a
woman who was stranded and
trying to signal for help. In the
end, 467,066 acres were lost,
much of it ponderosa pine, and
470 structures were destroyed

The Forest Fires

America is a nation with millions of acres of splendid wilderness, too much of which was lost as the West burned. California, New Mexico and Utah suffered immense blazes, while Colorado, Arizona and Oregon endured their largest-ever wildfires. Careless people were, as ever, part of the problem. But then there were the troubled ones, spreading mayhem in the time it takes to strike a match.

Jeff Topping/Reuters/Landov

H. Richardson/Denver Post/Gamma

A Hell of Our Own Making

"I'm shocked, and along with a lot of other people, in a state of disbelief." So said Rick Cables, a regional forester with the USDA Forest Service, after learning that 38-year-old Terry Lynn Barton, a part-time fire technician with the Service, had ignited a blaze on June 8 that would become the Hayman fire, the worst ever in Colorado, which sent acrid smoke wafting into Denver. In a bizarre saga, Barton said she put a match to an old letter from her estranged husband, then lost control of the situation and reported it as an abandoned campfire. When the fire was finally contained weeks later, 137,760 acres of National Forest had been razed and 600 structures lost. The mother and son above watch helplessly as their home is devoured, while at right, a courageous firefighter moves cautiously through the inferno created by one of his colleagues. As with any major forest fire, the area remains a dangerous place long after the fire itself is extinguished. Damaged trees present an ongoing hazard, and heavy rains can produce flooding and mudslides. Once-secure rocks may provide only treacherous footing.

Patrick Andrade/Gamma

M. Spencer Green/AP

A Challenging, Complex Battle

Much less acreage has been lost since WWII, at least partly because of today's aggressive techniques and the use of prescribed fires to eliminate fuel like brush and logs. Aircraft have played a vital role by sighting blazes, rushing in crews and dropping retardants like slurry (left). In these photos from Hayman, one group takes a breather, while another sizes up the damage. The severity of the western fires was due to drought and to a decline in prescribed fires—the result of revised policies, protests from some preservationists and from folks who have moved into the wilderness and prefer it pristine.

Ed Andrieski/AP (2)

PORTRAIT | The Osbournes

The most lovable madman ever to bite the head off a bird, Ozzy achieved crossover celebrity with a reality MTV show that touts good old family values: No (unsafe) sex, no drugs (look what they did to Dad!), and long live rock 'n' roll!

Neal Preston/Corbis

Appearances deceive: Back in the mid-'80s, when the Osbournes posed as shiny, happy people, Ozzy was an out-of-control wacko. Today, these latter-day Nelsons— or Simpsons, or Addamses—are the soul of normalcy.

In a previous life, Ozzy Osbourne was the singer in an apocalyptic British hard-rock band known as Black Sabbath. Then he was the solo artist behind such seminal works as *The Ultimate Sin, No Rest for the Wicked* and *Bark at the Moon.* He was a madman, and bloody well proud of it. His legendarily edgy performances were not confined to the studio and stage; on one occasion, during a high-toned lunch with an assemblage of recording industry suits, he did indeed bite the head off a nice little dove. In many or even most instances, Ozzy knew not what he did, being dead drunk, dangerously drugged or both.

Who knew that the Ozzman was only in rehearsal for his finest role, that of the 53-year-old put-upon patriarch of a way-nuclear family in an MTV reality television series? The pleasures of *The Osbournes* are several, from Jack and Kelly's very funny growing pains to mother Sharon's very frank modifiers, but it is Ozzy's guileless turn as a clueless multimillionaire recovering rock-god suburbanite that makes the show special. In a medium where nothing is new or different, *The Osbournes* is both, and it is a runaway hit, generating the highest ratings ever for a series on MTV.

A fascinating sidelight to the *Osbournes* phenomenon is how the show's success alters its interior reality. When we see Ozzy at the White House Correspondents dinner or Kelly launching her singing career with an instant hit (her ironic cover of Madonna's "Papa Don't Preach"), we can't be positive whether it's happening in real time or on the

MTV

The show (opposite, top) changed all reality for the family. Suddenly, the four Ozzies were celebs, ever in the glare of flashing cameras; Kelly was a budding pop star (below, on stage with Dad at the Rose Bowl in Pasadena) and Ozzy was certifiably mainstream. When he was awarded a star on the Walk of Fame in April (left), 1,000 adoring fans, many of whom never owned a Black Sabbath album, clogged Hollywood Boulevard.

Vinnie Zuffante/Gamma

Michael James/London Features

sitcom. And does it matter? It does, because we've come to care for the Osbournes. There's clearly a lot of love floating around that mansion, and since we believe in what we're seeing, the love matters to us in a way that "love" on, say, *Friends* or *8 Simple Rules for Dating My Teenage Daughter* never can.

This is important now, for Sharon is ill. The woman known only yesterday as a foul-mouthed tough cookie—the brains behind the Ozzfest tour (which grossed $25 million in the summer of 2002) and the one who squeezed MTV for up to $10 million for new episodes—might have been an unsympathetic figure in the show's sophomore season. But then we learned the plot twist: She's bravely battling colon cancer. If a Hollywood hack had come up with that, it would have seemed a contrived, desperate act. In reality, it is riveting, affecting drama.

Catuffe/Sipa

If at First . . .

Steve Fossett, the Chicago tycoon, always
had the will, and finally found a way. After
five failed attempts to make the first solo
balloon voyage around the world, he took
the low road over the Southern Hemisphere,
shaving more than 5,000 miles off a 25,000-
mile circumnavigation at the equator. Not
that he had things easy. He spent 13 frigid
days breathing through an oxygen mask
before spotting the finish line in Australia.
Then winds kept him from landing and he
spent an extra day aloft. When he finally
touched down on July 3, gusts dragged his
rig three miles across the desert. "Luckily,
the outback is a pretty big place," Fossett
said. "You don't run into many power lines."

Photograph by Collens Trevor
Marathon Racing/Gamma

Summer

Thrills—At a Terrible Cost

"I thought, It's flying too low over people. This is not a good stunt," said one spectator at an air show in July near Lviv, in western Ukraine. A Soviet-built SU-27 fighter jet was performing aerial acrobatics when it clipped the tops of trees, veered out of control, tore along the ground into onlookers—"They were cut down like grass"—then hit a plane on the ground and began to cartwheel (seen here) before bursting into a fireball and crashing into the crowded stands. At least 80 people died and well over a hundred were hurt.

Photograph by Oleg Nikishin Getty

July 4 Americans are not deterred from honoring the **nation's 226th birthday,** the first since the September 11 attacks. Las Vegas Mayor Oscar Goodman speaks for many celebrants when he says, "We're going to have our parades, we're going to have our symphonies, our concerts, and everyone's going to have a good time."

July 4 Armed with two guns and a six-inch knife, Egyptian-born Hesham Mohamed Ali Hadayet kills two Israelis at an El Al ticket counter in the **Los Angeles International Airport,** then is shot to death by security guards. Questions arise as to the prior handling of Hadayet's case by the INS.

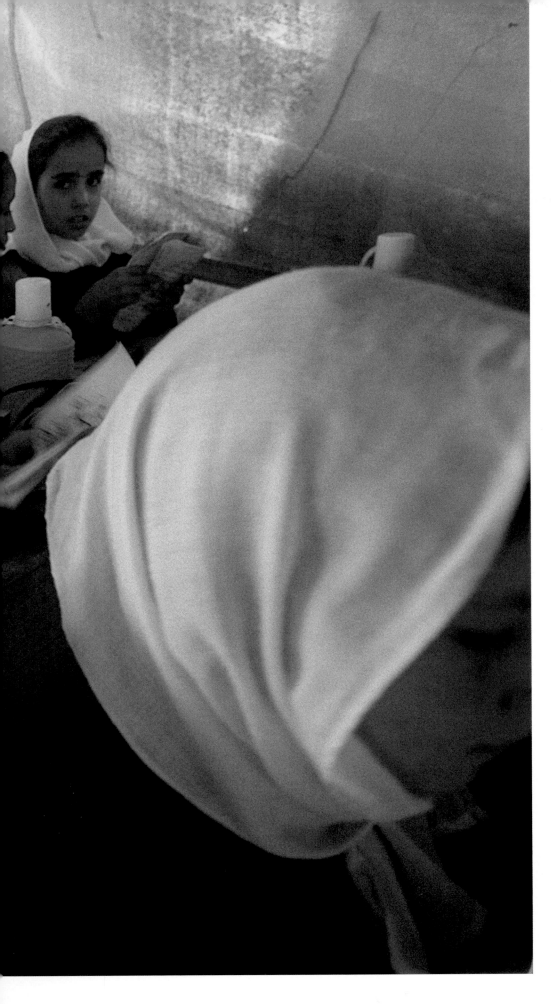

A New Semester

In July, 11-year-old Shabana Nabizada reads in her Kabul classroom. As the new school year got under way, many Afghan girls joined in for the first time: During the five years of Taliban rule, the education of women had been outlawed. While new opportunities were to be applauded, Afghan schools still faced serious problems. The Education Ministry appealed for $874 million to rebuild 2,500 schools and repair 3,500 others. And late in the year, a string of bombings and arson attacks near Kabul and to the south, where the Taliban had been strong, targeted girls' schools. The U.N. condemned the violence, adding, "We don't know who is responsible."

Photograph by Lynsey Addario
Corbis Saba

❝ These textbooks will teach tolerance. ❞

— **President Bush,** announcing a U.S. donation of millions of Pashto- and Dari-language textbooks to Afghan schools

July 9 A major study reveals that giving hormones to healthy postmenopausal women raises their risk of breast cancer, heart attacks, strokes and blood clots. Millions of women have been put on **hormone replacement therapy** to combat bone loss, heart disease and cancer.

July 9 Fans in Milwaukee boo when the All-Star Game, tied after 11 innings, ends because both teams **run out of pitchers.** Says Commissioner Bud Selig: "This is a very regrettable situation."

July 11 French scientists say they have found the skull, jawbone and teeth of a fossil perhaps **seven million years old** in a Chad desert. They call it "the oldest and most primitive known member of the hominid" family, but add that it is too soon to label it a direct ancestor of humans.

Gary Wathen/Reuters

To Hell and Back

A tale as tense as any thriller held the nation spellbound when nine coal miners were trapped 240 feet below the surface in a wet, freezing air pocket. The problems began on Wednesday, July 24, when their drill broke through into a long-abandoned shaft, and millions of gallons of water poured into their Somerset, Pa., mine. Fading hopes were buoyed on Thursday as a pipe began to pump warm air to the men. On Sunday morning, a nation thirsting for any good news awoke to learn that after 77 hours, all nine (above, Thomas Foy) had been lifted to safety. At left, a worker strains to hear the miners' voices.

Photograph Reuters/Landov

July 11 A team of U.S. scientists makes the first **synthetic virus** from scratch. Using mail-order material and a genetic blueprint from the Net, they create a polio virus.

July 21 Debt-ridden and reeling from an accounting fiasco, long-distance phone firm **WorldCom** (60,000 employees) files for the biggest bankruptcy in U.S. history.

On the Beach

Early on the morning of July 29, fifty-eight pilot whales were found stranded along Chapin Beach in the Cape Cod town of Dennis. Before the day was out, temperatures turned brutal and 11 of them died, despite the efforts of workers who covered the sunburned whales with sheets and doused them with water. Although low tide made it hard to get the creatures, which can weigh three tons, back into the sea, more than half were returned—only to beach themselves again. Some made it to the water a third time, and beached yet once more. These whales are extremely social mammals, and it's possible they followed their leader, who may have become disoriented. Certainly, by the end they were all in dire straits, and scientists had to euthanize 34 of them. Pilot whales have often had trouble in the area: In 1990, fifty-five were stranded. That year, two calves were rescued and released. In 2002, there were no survivors.

Photograph by Arnold Miller

Cape Cod Times/Gamma

❝ There were a lot of unfortunate factors. ❞

—**Teri Frady,** National Oceanic and Atmospheric Administration

July 24 Convicted of racketeering, bribery and corruption, **truculent Ohio Democrat** James Traficant is ousted from the House by a vote of 420–1, only the second such expulsion since the Civil War.

Aug. 4 Some float, some don't, in Darwin, Australia's 28th annual **Beer Can Regatta.** The only thing the unique ships have in common is that they are all made entirely from receptacles once used to hold suds.

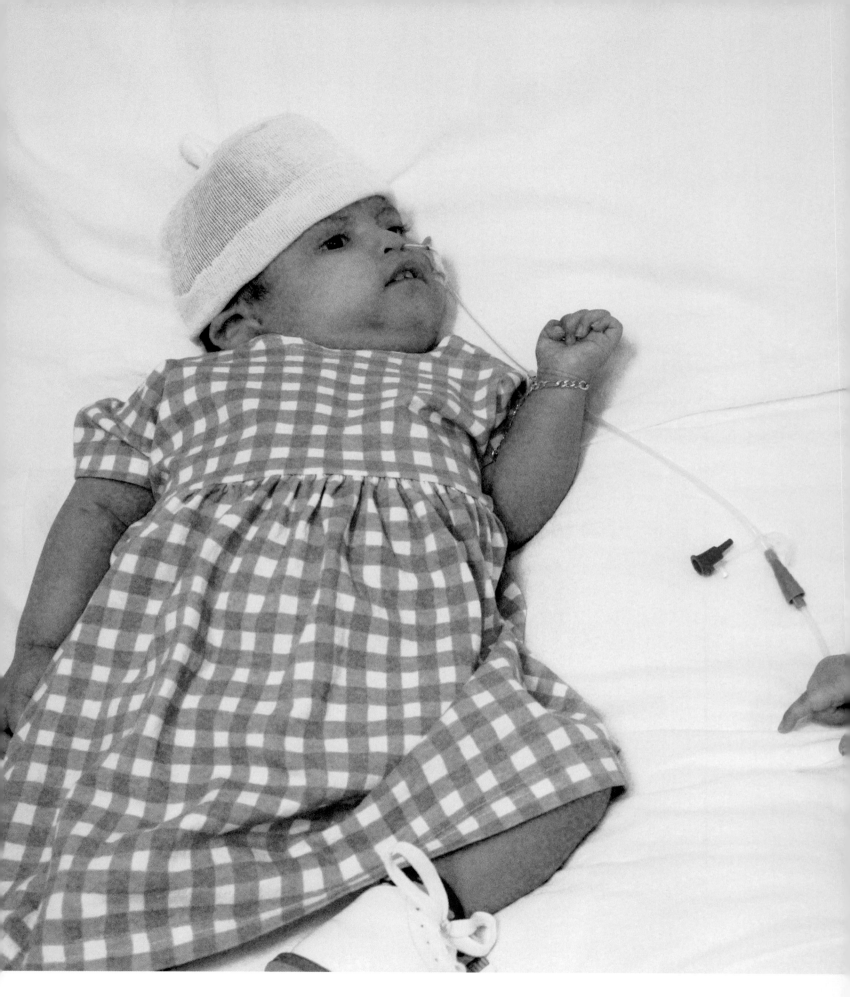

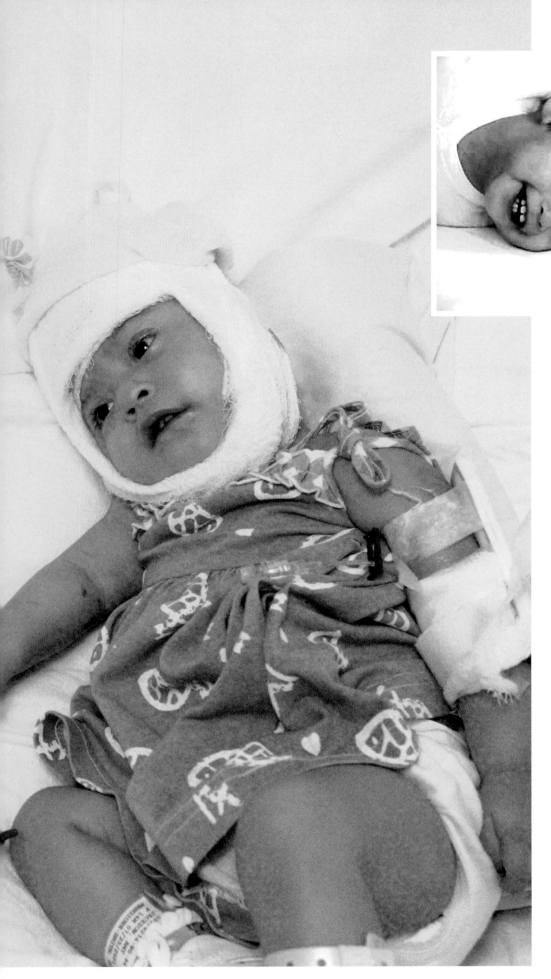

Amy Waddell/UCLA's Mattel Children's Hospital

How Nice to See You!

On July 25, 2001, a special event took place in Guatemala, something that happens just once in every 2.5 million births: Maria Teresa (left in both photos) and Maria de Jesus Quiej-Alvarez were born joined at the head. Their mother—who like many rural moms had no prenatal care—had endured an eight-day labor. The group Healing the Children stepped in, and a year later 50 doctors and nurses teamed at UCLA's Mattel Children's Hospital for a 22-hour operation to separate the girls. The lead surgeons predicted that by age five, the twins, who charmed everyone, would be leading normal lives.

Photograph by Scott Quintard
ASUCLA photo

Aug. 18 CNN televises **disturbing videos** allegedly made by al-Qaeda members that present "visual confirmation" of their plans for a global reign of terror. One tape shows the grisly death of a dog after a chemical gas is piped into an enclosure.

Aug. 22 Huge numbers of Chinese abandon their homes in Hunan Province as rivers and lakes swell to their highest levels in years. Says one official: "There are 900,000 people **fighting the floods.** There are people everywhere."

Storm over Europe

In August a low pressure front developed over England. That's not so unusual, but instead of moving northeast, the front drifted south, gathered moisture over the warm Mediterranean, then headed north. When it collided with cooler air, the seams burst and, for more than a week, a deluge fell in Central and Eastern Europe, bloating many rivers to historic levels. At least 100 lives were lost, and hundreds of thousands of people had to be evacuated. In Dresden, the Elbe rose above 30 feet for the first time. The autobahn between Munich and Salzburg (itself awash) was under as much as five feet of water. Bulgaria, Romania, Russia, Slovakia, all were hit hard, but none worse than the Czech Republic. Here, in Prague, the Vltava roils at 35 times the normal flow. Everywhere, damage was extensive, and officials fretted over the risk of tainted water supplies.

Photograph by Facelly Sipa

❝ The tragedy will not end with the retreat of the waters. It is a very difficult time ahead. ❞

—**John Sparrow,** International Red Cross

Aug. 25 Aaron Alvey and his Louisville teammates win the **Little League World Series** in Williamsport, Pa., beating Sendai, Japan, 1–0. The 12-year-old pitcher notches two Series records: 44 strikeouts and 21 consecutive scoreless innings.

Aug. 28 Divers locate a **Japanese midget submarine** three miles from Pearl Harbor, where, nearly 61 years ago, it was sunk an hour before the aerial attack began.

Sept. 8 "This one might take the cake," says 31-year-old Pete Sampras of his fifth U.S. Open **tennis crown** and his 14th Grand Slam title. He calls his win over Andre Agassi a "storybook ending."

Idolatry

"The good, the bad and the ugly—to the extreme." That's how Paula Abdul, a judge on *American Idol: The Search for a Superstar,* described the show. Apparently, much of America was willing to wade through a lot of bad and ugly performances each week during the long, hot summer as *Idol,* a *Star Search* for the new millennium, grew into a smash hit. It was finally determined that "good" was represented by frizzy-haired Pennsylvanian Justin Guarini (mouth agape) and big-voiced Texan Kelly Clarkson (all aswoon, center, after beating Guarini in the finals). "You sang your butt off," Abdul told her admiringly.

Photograph by Kevin Winter ImageDirect

Sept. 9 Contending that NASA staged the *Apollo 11* lunar landing, filmmaker/provocateur Bart Sibrel thrusts a Bible at astronaut Buzz Aldrin and challenges him to swear **he walked on the moon.** Rather than turn the other cheek, the 72-year-old Aldrin lets fly with a sock to the jaw.

Sept. 10 In a stunning development, actor and director Christopher Reeve, paralyzed since a 1995 horseback-riding accident, reveals that he is able to **move various parts of his body** and take a few steps in a pool. Reeve says that he's no Superman, but doctors believe the 50-year-old has accomplished something remarkable.

Sept. 11 On the first anniversary of the terrorist attacks, the winning New York State lottery numbers are **9-1-1.** Officials insist there was no patriotic hanky-panky.

9/11/02 in Pennsylvania

At 10:06 a.m., the time of day when, 365 days earlier, United Airlines Flight 93 crashed into this field in Somerset County, a large bell tolled 40 times and the names of 40 victims of the crash were read aloud. The memorial, called "A Time for Honor and Hope," featured speeches by politicians, friends and family of the deceased. "I cherish the memories of my sister and plan to work hard in school and in everything I do so she can be proud of me like I was of her," 11-year-old Murial Borza said of her big sister, Deora. Here, United flight attendants, many of them from Newark, N.J., where Flight 93 originated, support one another.

Photograph by Nina Berman Aurora

> **❝ Such an ugly thing to happen in such a beautiful place. ❞**
> —**Alice Hoglan,** mother of Mark Bingham, one of the Flight 93 passengers who stormed the cockpit on September 11

Sept. 14 Believed to be part of a terrorist "sleeper" cell, five men of Yemeni origin are arrested by the FBI in a Buffalo suburb, and days later another man is taken into custody. In October a federal grand jury indicts all six on charges that they were **trained at al-Qaeda camps** to support terrorist acts.

Sept. 14 Ten more fatalities are blamed on the **West Nile virus**, bringing the national total to 64. Late in the year the death toll climbs to 214 out of 3,737 reported cases.

Sept. 25 Bell Labs fires Jan Hendrik Schön, 32, after an investigation finds that **the physicist had fabricated data** for his astonishing work in molecular electronics. A Nobel Prize had seemed in the offing.

FOCUS ON 9/11/02 in NYC

One of the most prestigious photography seminars is the annual Barnstorm conference, better known as "the Eddie Adams workshop." Each year since 1988, the Pulitzer Prize–winning Adams has hosted 100 deserving photographers for a weekend at his upstate–New York spread. There, they learn from the best: Kennerly, Mark, Towell, Adams himself. For Barnstorm XV, Adams—precisely one year after September 11—led his amateurs and professionals to the city. A sample of the rich results, which can and will fill a book (to be published in 2003), may be seen here. "I wanted to do something to show the resilient spirit of New Yorkers," says Adams, "to show the bad guys they are now history."

On the Subway *Ted McLaren*

Manhattan Skyline *Chris Ramirez*

Waking *Sheila Masson*

Sunrise *Pete Souza*

Morning Exercise *Susana Bates*

Grand Central Terminal *David Hume Kennerly*

Staten Island Ferry *David Y. Lee*

Brooklyn Bridge *Daniel Myles Cullen*

Ground Zero
David Turnley

Memorial *Chris Lopez*

Ground Zero
Thomas E. Franklin

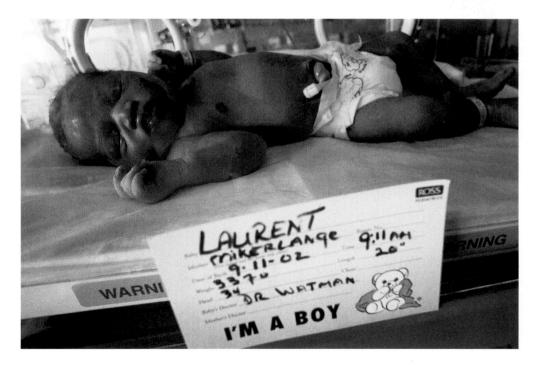

Newborn *Julia Xanthos*

Bride-to-be *Dana Fineman-Appel*

A Song for New York *Larry Towell*

Visitors from England *Garth Vaughan*

Taking Pictures *Mary Ellen Mark*

Flagwaving
Jonathan Kirshner

Kiss
Sandra Liebig

Prayer
Kristine Nyborg

Prayer
Gunes Kocatepe

Prayer
Rhonda Yeager

PORTRAIT Keiko

The celebrity orca better known by his *nom de cine,* Willy, swam back into the picture when he cozied up to new chums in Norway, boosting his reputation as the friendliest fella ever to sport fins.

Always ready for his close-up, Keiko turns on the charm in the Skaalvik fjord. The recalcitrant cutup delights the locals even as he disappoints his rehabilitators.

Gorm Kallestad/Scanpix

Gary Braasch

Michael Melford

The world's most put-upon, controversy-plagued sea mammal had another stressful year in the spotlight, though he again let the hullabaloo slide off his back like so much water. Everyone's always blubbering over Keiko—everyone, that is, but Keiko.

You remember Keiko? "Willy?" He who would be free? That's him. Keiko was the real-life killer whale who played Willy in three popular 1990s movies. Of course, "real life" is a subjective term, and Keiko's existence has rarely resembled that of an everyday orca. This, always, has been the rub.

Keiko's saga begins in the North Atlantic. There, in 1979, a two-year-old killer whale was captured

and eventually sold into the theme-park trade. Without apparent irony, he was given the stage name Keiko, Japanese for Lucky One. He performed in pools in Canada and Mexico for years before gaining Hollywood fame in 1993's *Free Willy*.

By 1996 activists who had been seeking to unpen Keiko carried the day, and long-term plans were sketched for the whale's reintroduction to the wild. First, Keiko was transferred from a Mexican amusement park to the Oregon Coast Aquarium for rehab. Then in 1998 he was airlifted back to Iceland, where, in a large sea pen, he was taught to catch fish and, it was hoped, fend for himself. After four years of training, he was thought ready for the open ocean and was released in July 2002. The idea

The inappropriateness of a captive whale playing a liberated one wasn't lost on activists who, with Keiko's screen bow in 1993, began spouting off. Their campaign led to the longest, strangest trip ever swum by an orca: From Mexican pool to Oregon aquarium to a huge sling used in the airlift to Iceland.

Bob Talbot

was that he would join a group of orcas—they forage in packs—and live to a ripe old age.

What happened next would make a good movie, albeit a politically incorrect one. Six weeks after his release, Keiko showed up in a Norwegian bay where he proceeded to delight the townsfolk of Halsa with his old vaudeville antics. He leapt and played in the Skaalvik fjord as the locals came close, then closer. "He is completely tame and he clearly wants company," said Arild Birger Neshaug, who was out rowing with his 12-year-old daughter, Hanne, and her friends when he spotted Keiko in early September. "At first we were skeptical, and then we tried petting his back. Finally the children went swimming with him." Tourists flocked to Halsa, a village 250

miles northwest of Oslo, as yet another ironic chapter was written in Keiko's ironic life story: He became beloved in a nation that commercially hunts whales despite a global ban.

Not all Norwegians were amused. Nils Oien of the Institute of Marine Research in Bergen created a squall when he asserted, "This is all madness. First they spend millions on training him and turning him into a movie star. Then they spend more millions on turning him back into a wild animal. They should have let him live and die in captivity. Now that they have decided not to keep him in captivity, they should put him down." His comments were called "absurd and shortsighted" by the Humane Society of the United States, and Keiko's sponsors

insisted that their orca had passed a first test of natural living by traveling the nearly 900 miles to Norway without losing a pound.

But even they weren't happy about Keiko's apparent regression to his showbiz days and ways. They quickly made plans to move him yet again, to Taknes Bay, six miles from Halsa, where cleaner, less busy water was available. They asked all Norwegians to please steer clear of Keiko for his own sake. Finally, they pointed out that Taknes is visited by wild orcas in midwinter, and reiterated their hope that Keiko would reenlist with his own kind.

Only one thing was certain as the credits rolled: In finest Tinseltown tradition, there are bound to be yet more sequels.

Chuck Davis

Gorm Kallestad/Scanpix

Chuck Davis

The star of three *Willy* films was himself set free off Iceland (above, wearing his transmitter), having completed retraining that included "walks" in the wild (left). The plan was for Keiko to retire among his own, munching herring and telling thrilling tales of his remarkable life. Instead, he prefers to shine in Halsa (right).

A Blast from On High

No one or no thing had a more active autumn than Sicily's Old Faithful, Mount Etna, the largest and most volatile volcano in Europe. On October 27, this year's series of eruptions, among Etna's fiercest in recent times, began—then continued for weeks. Lava flows gobbled up power lines and a host of small buildings at a tourist complex. Here, in a satellite image taken shortly after Etna started to blow, plumes of smoke stream south, away from Italy's boot and out over the Mediterranean.

Photograph by NASA

Fall

The Aroma of Scandal

In fashioning a career that has brought her oodles of money, Martha Stewart has instructed a nation of eager disciples in new and improved ways to live their lives, to cook, to clean, to garden, to employ seashells precisely as she did with those she selected (casually but with a clever eye) on the Seychelles. Then the world learned at midyear that she may have been involved in selling stock on an illegal insider basis. Here, in October, she leaves her office on the day she resigned her seat on the stock exchange. Nearly every aspect of her business has been hurt (Kmart is the only sizable exception), and she has lost $300 million. Whether Martha would do jail time was the watercooler question of the year, as her deriders—and she attracts them like flies—imagined all the good things she could do with stripes.

Photograph by William Miller Sipa

❝ We were very encouraged that people are separating Martha Stewart Living the brand from Martha Stewart the personality. ❞

—**James Adamson,** CEO of Kmart

Oct. 9 Saying the labor dispute "imperils our national health and safety," President Bush invokes the Taft-Hartley Act and **orders longshoremen back to work** after a 10-day lockout that idled 200 ships in 29 West Coast ports.

Oct. 11 Jimmy Carter, the 39th U.S. President, wins the Nobel Peace Prize for his "untiring effort to find **peaceful solutions** to international conflicts."

Oct. 13 In the **largest meat recall** in U.S. history, Wampler pulls 27.4 million pounds of cooked poultry off the shelf since it may carry listeria, a dangerous bacteria strain.

PRET
hand made, natural food, avoiding
obscure chemicals, additives
and preservatives common
to so much of the
'prepared' and 'fast'
food on the market today.
LADS ★ JUICES ★ CAKES

O Beauteous, Hateful Isle

Bali is a place most folks can only dream of seeing. Then there are the lucky ones who actually visit the Pacific paradise. Tom Singer, the 17-year-old Australian at left, was on his first-ever trip outside his country. He had worked hard baby-sitting and in a shop to earn money for what would be a once-in-a-lifetime experience. On Saturday, October 12, the lad was enjoying himself at a popular club when a car bomb went off, killing some 180 people. Here, Hannabeth Luke, an Australian surfer whose boyfriend died in the blast, helps Tom flee the site. A month later, he was dead of his injuries. A week after that, Iman Samudra, an Afghan-trained militant with alleged links to al-Qaeda, was arrested for masterminding the act.

Photograph by Maldonado Roberto
Gamma

Oct. 15 A check for $1.4 million from Polish immigrant Joe Temeczko is sent to New York City in honor of 9/11. **The self-employed handyman,** who died at the age of 86 a month after the attacks, had included the gift in his will. No one knows how he amassed such a sum.

Oct. 20 In an effort to buttress internal support as he faces a possible invasion, Saddam Hussein **empties Iraq's jails,** freeing tens of thousands of inmates.

Oct. 31 Aftershocks hamper rescuers as an earthquake in southern Italy **traps 56 schoolchildren;** 26 of the kids, and a teacher, die. Three days later, a massive earthquake—7.9—rocks interior Alaska.

Nov. 1 **"The Queen came through for me,"** says Paul Burrell when he is acquitted of charges that he stole some 300 items from Princess Diana's estate. The trial ends after Queen Elizabeth says that the former butler had told her he was safekeeping Di's belongings.

The Ball Is Handed Down

Over the course of several summer days, the St. Louis Cardinals confronted two deaths in the family: The team's beloved radio voice, Jack Buck, 77, lost his battle with lung cancer, and, shockingly, pitcher Darryl Kile died in his sleep at age 33. The cause, in a man whose family had a history of heart disease, was an 80-to-90 percent blockage of the coronary artery. The Cardinals were staggered, but regrouped and, freshly inspired, raced into the postseason as baseball's hottest team. Here, on October 12, prior to Game Three of their playoff series against the San Francisco Giants, Cards players flank Kile's five-year-old son, Kannon, as the national anthem plays. The Giants eliminated the Cardinals, then were themselves beaten by the Anaheim Angels in a wild World Series.

Photograph by Julie Jacobson AP

❝ It's like a dark cloud is hanging over this city. ❞

—**Ron Noll,** Cardinals fan, when Darryl Kile's death followed that of Jack Buck

Nov. 5 The GOP regains the Senate and adds to its House majority in stunning **midterm elections.** Main factors include Democratic apathy, the war on terrorism and a campaign blitz by President Bush.

Nov. 6 Actress Winona Ryder, 31, is convicted of grand theft and vandalism for **shoplifting** $5,560 worth of merchandise from a Beverly Hills Saks Fifth Avenue.

Nov. 8 After five days, leukemia survivor Lloyd Scott clumps across the finish line of the New York City Marathon. Wearing a 130-pound **antique diving outfit,** the former English fireman raised money to battle the disease and to aid families of firefighters lost on September 11. Scott also wanted to demonstrate what a cancer victim is able to accomplish.

NTV Russian Channel/Sipa

Russian Roulette

"I swear by God we are more keen on dying than you are keen on living," said a Chechen rebel in a tape made before 41 guerrillas stormed a Moscow theater on October 23 and took hostage the 800 attendees who had been watching a hit musical. The rebels had wrapped themselves in explosives (above), and said they would blow up the theater if President Vladimir Putin refused to withdraw Russian forces from the separatist Chechnya province. After 57 hours of drama, fentanyl, a potent narcotic, was piped into the building, leading to the deaths of all the militants—and 123 of the hostages. Doctors claimed they could have saved more lives had the authorities not concealed the identity of the gas for four days.

Photograph by Vladimir Sichov Sipa

Nov. 13 "Yes, it is his voice," says a State Department official about a tape of Osama bin Laden extolling terrorist acts and promising **spectacular new attacks.**

Nov. 19 A tanker with **twice as much oil** as the *Exxon Valdez* breaks in two and sinks off Spain. Most of the oil was trapped in compartments, and may gel in the chilly depths, but only time will tell.

Day of the Tornadoes

October 24: Three tornadoes cause one death and some 30 injuries in Corpus Christi, Tex. October 28: A tornado in Chataignier, La., heaves a mobile home 200 yards, killing two and injuring five. November 5: A tornado rips through Abbeville, Ala., killing one and injuring 31. But all that was only a drumbeat to November 10, when 88 twisters touched down in a swath that extended from Louisiana to Pennsylvania, killing at least 35 people and injuring scores more. In eastern Tennessee, the hamlets of Mossy Grove and Petros were all but obliterated. Here, a tornado rolls through Tiffin, Ohio, leaving shattered homes in its wake.

Photograph by Allan Detrich
The Toledo Blade

" I said, 'Please, God, don't let this be happening,' and by the time I said 'happening,' it was over. "

—**Art Bowman,** Coffee County, Tennessee

Nov. 19 Congress approves a Homeland Security Department to fight terrorism. The legislation calls for the **largest federal reorganization** in 50 years.

Nov. 21 Princess Anne becomes the first modern British royal to be convicted of a crime after her bullterrier, Dotty, attacks two children. Anne is fined and pays $393 in compensation, but **the dog's life is spared** as the judge rules that "the owners are extremely responsible."

Nov. 21 U.S. officials reveal that Abd al-Rahim al-Nashiri, a senior al-Qaeda leader, has been captured. Al-Nashiri, a Saudi who seems to harbor **a hatred for the U.S. Navy,** is believed to have planned the 1998 embassy bombings, the 2000 attack on the USS *Cole* and similar acts.

A Long Winter's Nap

With her beard a-drooping and her cap adrift, Samantha Hall of Australia catches 40 well-earned winks on the shoulder of Brooklynite Luna McIntyre as a bus takes them to their next Sidewalk Santa gig. Hall, McIntyre and their fellow elves had earlier been schooled in proper Santa-logical deportment at a daylong seminar aboard the World Yacht's *Princess.* ("Don't eat garlic or raw onions before taking your post," counseled guest instructor Skitch Henderson of the New York Pops.) This December's was the 100th Yuletide that the Volunteers of America's cast of Kringles collected donations on the streets of the city, their efforts this time helping feed more than 6,600 needy people.

Photograph by Jay L. Clendenin Polaris

Dec. 2 Former CBS chief executive Thomas H. Wyman, in an interview with *The New York Times,* calls the Augusta National Golf Club's no-women-members stance **"pigheaded."** A week earlier the 25-year member had resigned from the club. Augusta's Masters tournament has been televised by CBS for 46 years.

Dec. 3 Police say that 23 women have been attacked in Suwa, a town 100 miles northwest of Tokyo, by a **rogue monkey.** The swinger, likely a Japanese macaque, is thought to have employed the gorilla tactics in his heated search for a mate.

Dec. 4 Three more men are detained by Kenyan authorities, bringing to more than a dozen the number of suspects being questioned in the Nov. 28 attacks on Israelis. At least 15 died when a car bomb went off outside the Paradise Hotel, near Mombasa. Only minutes earlier two heat-seeking missiles barely missed an Israeli charter plane that took off not far away, raising concerns in the United States about **how to defend domestic flights** against such shoulder-launched weapons. Evidence ties al-Qaeda to the assaults.

FOCUS ON "The Sniper"

In a country beset by the fear of slaughter without warning, the last thing any community needed was to fall into the grip of a maniac who executes people with no regard for race, color or creed. Even a child wasn't safe. This was the nightmare that seized the Washington, D.C., area when "the sniper" went stalking.

Bill Cornett/Gamma

Initial Impact

The opening volley in the 22-day siege pierces the window of an arts and crafts store in the Washington suburb of Aspen Hill, Md., on October 2. This bullet strikes no one, but in less than an hour a man is shot dead 3.6 miles away in a supermarket parking lot (above). On the next day, five more lives will be taken, four in Maryland, one in D.C.

Robert Trippett/Sipa

Matthew Cavanaugh/AP

The Banality of Evil

That people were being gunned down in the midst of ordinary day-to-day activities lent a nasty, surreal edge to the ordeal. Gas stations (the site of four killings) and shopping areas were sniper magnets. Many folks, heeding tips on concealment they got from TV, chose to get a few dollars' worth rather than fill it up. Above: A tarp is strung at this Virginia station to provide some sense of security. At top right, police in Falls Church, Va., search for clues after a woman was slain

Doug Mills/AP

Michael Williamson/The Washington Post

Jim Bourg/Reuters/Landov

as she and her husband were putting purchases in the trunk of their car. At left, Sonia Wills has just learned that her son, a 35-year-old father of two, is dead. Everyone was asking the same questions: Why is it happening? How many snipers are there? How can such a massive manhunt be getting nowhere? The buck stopped with Montgomery County (Md.) Police Chief Charles Moose (right), 49, who was under intense heat. At first, some scoffed at his methods; Moose would prove them wrong.

A Coast-to-Coast Spree?

Each of 13 D.C.-area shootings, which claimed 10 lives, involved one bullet (a sniper's motto: One shot, one kill). When two males were arrested on October 24, one was Army Gulf War vet John Allen Muhammad (above, in the Louisiana National Guard), 41, an expert marksman. He hooked up with John Lee Malvo, 17, in 2001. They drifted across the U.S. as father and son (right, in July 2002), killing as they went, authorities determined.

Polaris (2)

Brandan McDermid/Reuters/Landov

The End of the Road Brings Welcome Relief

The phantom of the manhunt was "the white van." Widespread searches brought traffic to a standstill, but with no luck. Then the search turns to—and finds—the Chevy Caprice above, with Muhammad and Malvo asleep inside, along with a Bushmaster .223 rifle that fits the crimes. The car has been altered so a sniper can operate from the trunk. Below: The next day, a thankful community returns to normal.

Robert A. Martin/AP

PORTRAIT | Halle Berry

The actress from the heartland had a monster year, shattering precedent at the Oscars, making a splash as the Bond girl to end all Bond girls. With her personal life, too, going swimmingly, the lovely Berry is no longer Jinxed.

Before acting or modeling, she was a beauty queen, winning the 1986 Miss Teen Ohio pageant, then finishing second at Miss U.S.A. and third in Miss World. Her biggest title by far, presented to her by bad boy Russell Crowe, was Oscar-winner.

The daughter of a black father who abandoned the family and a white mother who made ends meet as a nurse, young Halle Berry didn't have it easy growing up in the Cleveland suburbs. Beyond her family's struggles, she remembers being teased at school, and the Oreo cookie left in her mailbox. When she was almost elected her high school's prom queen, she was accused of stuffing the ballot box. "That's when it hit me," she told *Premiere* magazine in 1995. "They like me until I'm representing a symbol of beauty in our school."

They're not making fun of her anymore. Berry, 36, has risen beyond her beauty-pageant and Midwest modeling careers (at five foot seven, she was too short for the catwalks of New York or Milan) to the heights of stardom. In March she became the first woman of color to win the Best Actress Academy Award for her role in the edgy *Monster's Ball;* she also, with Denzel Washington, was part of the first African American duo to sweep the top categories. "This moment is so much bigger than me," an overcome Berry said when, at last, she found her voice. "This moment is for the women who stand before me . . . for every woman of color who now has a chance as the door has been opened."

It certainly wasn't clear theretofore that Berry was a candidate for crusader. Trying to move from modeling in Chicago to acting in New York, she found herself sleeping in a homeless shelter and then at the Y. When she did land a role, it was on the deservedly forgotten sitcom *Living Dolls.* Trying L.A., she got a recurring part on the soap *Knots Landing,* and then, in 1991, a break when she won the role of a crack addict in Spike Lee's *Jungle Fever.*

Philip Ramey

AP

Keith Hamshere/United Artists

The men in her life: Benét consoles Berry as they walk from her lawyer's office in L.A. a week after the car crash; Justice and his wife attend an Atlanta seminar on violence in 1993; and, of course, Bond—James Bond.

Her profile in the celebrity pages was also boosted when she wed star baseball player David Justice in 1993. They divorced in 1997, and two years later she became secretly engaged to jazz musician Eric Benét. He was at her side during the difficult days of February 2000, after Berry left the scene of a car accident. She said that, having whacked her head, she didn't remember speeding off, but she was fined $13,500, was put on probation and was hit with a lawsuit by the other driver.

There was no predicting Berry's future—superstar? sexpot? tabloid fodder?—before *Monster's Ball.* Now all is clear. She will continue to accept challenging roles, of which there will be no shortage, meantime appearing in blockbusters on the scale of the latest James Bond smash, *Die Another Day.* Berry made such an impression opposite Pierce Brosnan that there are plans to honor the superspy Jinx with her own sequel—the first spin-off in Bond franchise history, and another first from Halle Berry.

LIFE Remembers

From Barbie to Bugs Bunny, from royals to rockers, from makers of film noir to makers of first downs, they presented us with a thousand reasons for laughing and crying, for considering and reconsidering—and sometimes, simply, a way in which to understand ourselves a little better. Lawbreaker, lawmaker, pint-size, robust, clown, adventurer: These people lived lives that touched ours.

Milton Berle

Known as Mr. Television, he personally ushered the new medium to a level of must-see, must-have. Born in 1908, Berle entered show biz at the age of five and continued working for the rest of the century. At six he was in his first movie; he played the Palace Theatre in '31 and for decades worked radio and the vaudeville circuit like a man—or a woman—possessed. In 1948, when he started his variety show, the visual gags and props went boffo on TV, and the nation tuned in to Mr. Tuesday Night. When his antics lost their allure, Uncle Miltie settled into a career of guest shots and big cigars.

Cecil Beaton

The Queen Mother

The tininess, the sweet, constant smile, the colorful dresses and fanciful hats, the vibrant old age that carried her all the way to 101—these combined to make her, as the famous photographer of royalty Cecil Beaton put it, "the great mother figure and nanny of us all." But beneath the image was a woman of steel. She helped her husband, the reluctant monarch King George VI, buck up the empire during the darkest days of World War II, then helped her family through its recent episodes of tragedy and scandal. "For me, she meant everything," said her grandson Prince Charles. "I had dreaded, dreaded this moment."

Cecil Beaton/Camera Press/Retna

Princess Margaret

Whether she simply missed out on her mother's gene for extraordinary longevity or was felled by too many years of cigarettes and Famous Grouse whisky, Margaret, the playful younger daughter of Albert, Duke of York, and Lady Elizabeth Bowes-Lyon (later the Queen Mum), died, frail and nearly blind, at 71. She was, from the get-go, the party-girl foil to her sister Elizabeth's somber queen-in-waiting persona. "Disobedience is my joy!" exclaimed the petite beauty as she galavanted about swinging '60s London, strewing tabloid headlines in her wake. Her impetuous love affairs and failed marriage to Lord Snowdon brought her criticism from the upper crust, but those who knew Margaret well knew her as generous, smart, kind—and a royal lot of fun.

Walter Iooss Jr./Sports Illustrated

John Unitas

He was the last of the old school and the first of the new, a stony-faced quarterback with a liquid nitrogen grasp of a gladiators' game going space-age. When he came to pro football, they said he didn't have the arm or the legs. But he had two things they couldn't see: the biggest heart in the game, and a field vision that made everything look slo-mo. In 1958 he essentially invented the two-minute drill as he led the Colts to victory over the Giants in an overtime tilt that made TV gaga for the NFL. Unfortunately, the strong heart finally gave out. Johnny U. was 69.

Ted Williams

Possessing extraordinary senses, he was able to see the seam on an 80-mph curveball or hear a heckler 300 feet away. A man of many nicknames—Teddy Ballgame, the Splendid Splinter, the Kid—Williams was a pure hitter and, during his career with the Boston Red Sox, a prickly character. All he wanted was to be deemed the best batsman ever, but John Glenn, his squad leader during the Korean War, remembered him as the best wingman he ever flew with, while angling buddies in Florida recalled him as the best fisherman ever to bait a hook. The last man to hit .400 in a season died at age 83.

Seattle Slew

The black stallion, horse racing's last living Triple Crown winner, cantered to the ripe old age of 28 before crossing the finish line at Hill 'n' Dale farm in Lexington, Ky., in May. Slew passed away on the 25th anniversary of his Kentucky Derby win, a triumph that spurred his run through the Preakness and Belmont Stakes to the sport's most bejeweled crown. Equally as impressive at stud, Slew sired 102 stakes winners who earned more than $75 million in purses. "He had a good life," Seattle Slew's jockey Jean Cruguet said. "He did everything a horse could do."

Sam Snead

As a boy on the family farm in Virginia, young Sammy would take a tree branch, make himself a club of sorts and go around swiping at rocks. Or so goes the legend regarding the genesis of what matured into the sweetest swing golf has ever known. "Any guy who would pass up a chance to see Snead on a golf course," the sportswriter Jim Murray once opined, "would pull the shades driving past the Taj Mahal." A pro star from the 1930s into the '60s, and a Hall of Fame yarn-spinner even longer, the storied Slammin' Sam finally posted his scorecard at age 89.

Hy Peskin

Susan CopenOken/Sports Illustrated

Bettmann/Corbis

Richard Helms

The quintessential superspook was born to money in St. Davids, Pa., in 1913. Schooled in Switzerland for two years, he learned to speak French and German; during WWII, these skills took him to the OSS, the precursor to the CIA. Helms stayed on, and got noticed in '55 when he ran a 500-foot tunnel into East Berlin that let the agency eavesdrop there for nearly a year. In 1966 he became the first career officer to take the reins in Langley and served till '73, when he was forced out by President Nixon, who was piqued that Helms refused to help in the Watergate cover-up. In 1977, Helms drew a suspended sentence for lying to Congress about the CIA's dealings in Chile. Said Helms, "I had sworn my oath to protect certain secrets."

Abba Eban

As important as anyone to the birth of Israel, he moved with his family to England as a baby and went on to be a bright light at Cambridge. With British Intelligence during World War II, he served in Egypt and Palestine and, already immersed in Zionism, became devoted to the notion of Israeli statehood. His fiery speech before the U.N. in 1947 helped secure that independence, and paved the way to his becoming, as David Ben-Gurion put it, "the voice of the Hebrew nation." In the end, his dovishness, intellectual éclat, three-piece suits and command of 10 languages—in a land where soft politics and smooth polish are somewhat suspect—may have prevented him from achieving his ultimate goal, that of prime minister.

Paul Wellstone

On October 25, a campaign plane crashed in northern Minnesota, killing everyone aboard: Democratic Senator Paul Wellstone, his wife of 39 years, Sheila (seen here with her husband at the Vietnam Memorial in Washington, D.C.), their daughter Marcia, three campaign aides and two pilots. In the resulting tumult of a new, weeklong campaign, former U.S. Vice President Walter F. Mondale agreed to pick up the Wellstone banner, but then was beaten by Republican Norm Coleman. A memorial service for Wellstone that devolved into a rally was a turning point. Lost in the frenzy of posthumous politics was Wellstone the man: friendly, engaged, caring, dedicated to principle and task.

Joey McLeister/Star Tribune

John Gotti

The last of the celebrity mafiosi, the Dapper Don differed from most thugs in that he courted the attention. Asked by his future Judas, Salvatore "Sammy Bull" Gravano, if he was bothered by people staring, he said, "This is my public, Sammy. They love me." Gotti rose from heading a Brooklyn teen gang, the Fulton-Rockaway Boys, to the Gambino crime family, which he took over in '85 when he had Paul Castellano gunned down in the street. While the tabloids cooed TEFLON DON, he beat a string of charges, but in 1992, murder and racketeering finally stuck. He spent the rest of his days in a six-by-eight cell until he died of cancer at 61.

Byron White

A quintessential American success story, he rose to fame as a three-sport star at Colorado, graduated first in his class and became a Rhodes Scholar. In 1940 he scored the highest grades at Yale Law School while leading the National Football League in rushing for a second time. In naval intelligence during WWII, he won two Bronze Stars. In 1962 he began a 31-year stint on the Supreme Court, where his fierce privacy and independence riled some. Democrats felt betrayed when the man appointed by JFK as "the ideal New Frontier judge" ruled conservatively; Republicans couldn't trust him because he was JFK's man. His great speed on the gridiron saddled him with the nickname he never liked. When asked in Washington in 1961, "Aren't you 'Whizzer' White?" he replied, "I was." He was 84.

Haji Abdul Qadir

In July, a hail of bullets cut down Vice President Qadir in downtown Kabul, shaking Afghanistan's transitional U.S.-backed government. As a Pashtun moderate, the former mujahedin commander had been a key ally of President Hamid Karzai—who was himself nearly assassinated in September. A controversial figure, Qadir, born circa 1954, had enemies that included the Taliban (who executed his brother in 2001), al-Qaeda and a variety of Northern Alliance and tribal leaders. Eyewitnesses saw two gunmen get away by taxi. The usual suspects, his bodyguards, were detained.

Allan Grant

Loomis Dean

Billy Wilder

His mother, who loved all things American, gave him his nickname
in honor of Buffalo Bill. Born in what was then Austria-Hungary,
Wilder was already a veteran of the German cinema when he went
to Hollywood to escape the Nazis, bringing with him a worldly
view spiked with a stiletto humor that tore through his writing
and directing. Lye-soaked phrases, gimlet observations and ribald
impudence defined his films, whether the noir classic *Double
Indemnity* or the weltschmerz-riddled *Ace in the Hole*. And yet,
the man's films never failed to entertain. *Witness for the
Prosecution* uncorked one surprise after another; *Sunset
Boulevard* hypnotized as it devastated. Wilder was 95.

John Frankenheimer

This New Yorker learned filmmaking with the Motion Picture
Squadron of the U.S. Air Force, then reached his artistic peak with
a chilling tale of cold war conspiracies. In just two years, 1961 and
'62, three films that would secure Frankenheimer's fame were
released: *The Young Savages, Birdman of Alcatraz* (both starring
Burt Lancaster) and, most important, *The Manchurian Candidate*.
That dark depiction of an assassination plot took on an eerie
afterglow when the director's close friend, President John F.
Kennedy, was killed in 1963. JFK's death sent Frankenheimer into
an alcoholic spiral, but he enjoyed a renaissance with several
acclaimed films on cable TV in the '90s. He died at 72 of a stroke.

James Coburn

He was one of those king-size American actors bred to ride the range on the big screen, though he saddled up in scores of TV oaters before making a name in *The Magnificent Seven* in 1960. Coburn (right) also had an unmistakable savvy, a lusty grin and a why-not attitude perfect for the self-conscious hedonism of the '60s—as in the 007 spoof *Our Man Flint* and *The President's Analyst.* He starred in other flicks, but mostly he worked as a supporting actor, for which he copped an Oscar in 1997's *Affliction.* He was on the mend from two decades of rheumatoid arthritis when a heart attack stopped him at age 74.

Harry Benson

Bill Ray

Richard Harris

A son of Limerick, he fit right in with a generation of gifted Anglo-Irish actor-boozers. Tall, sinewy, rough-hewn, he was born to play the explosive miner-turned-rugby-star in 1963's *This Sporting Life.* Some fine parts followed, in *Hawaii, Camelot* and *A Man Called Horse,* but ensuing flops mixed with excesses left him in the '80s touring in *Camelot* for three years. Then the '90s brought a star turn in *The Field,* solid supporting roles and raves for his West End work in Pirandello's *Henry IV,* all capped off by a gift for his granddaughter— the role of Professor Dumbledore in the two *Harry Potter* hits. He died of cancer at 72.

Kim Hunter

The former Janet Cole trained at the Actors Studio, and was already a respected up-and-comer when she originated the role of Stella Kowalski in Tennessee Williams's *A Streetcar Named Desire* on Broadway in 1947. She was teamed with fellow Method thespian Marlon Brando, and when the pair reprised their roles in the 1951 film, both were nominated for Oscars; Hunter won Best Supporting Actress. Her career was all but ended shortly thereafter when she was blacklisted during the Communist witch-hunts. She returned later in life to entertain a new generation, monkeying around thrice in the *Planet of the Apes* movies. Kim Hunter was 79.

Rod Steiger

He brought a new intensity to the screen, welding the Method to a machine-gun delivery punctuated by a half moan, half roar that made clear anything and everything might be about to break loose. In *The Big Knife, The Pawnbroker, In the Heat of the Night,* something profound yet primordial emerges. It wounds, then cauterizes, only that it may wound again. Steiger (right), who died at 77, was unyielding in his search for honesty. "I'm 60 percent virgin and 40 percent whore," he said in 2000. "I've not sold out that much, and I've made my own mistakes."

Kobal

Everett Collection

Lawrence Tierney

There is a scene in a kitchen in 1947's *Born to Kill* where a guy wises off to Lawrence Tierney. It is quite frightening because Tierney was the sort whose path you didn't want to cross, let alone provoke while in a confined area. This went for offscreen, as well, where he specialized in headline-making bar brawls. His career certainly wasn't helped when he ripped a public phone off the wall, or when he smashed a waiter in the face with a sugar bowl, or when he got himself stabbed. Still, he mesmerized in *Dillinger, The Devil Thumbs a Ride* and Quentin Tarantino's *Reservoir Dogs.* Tierney (left) was 82. As for the guy in the kitchen? He died too.

Dudley Moore

Growing up near London, he was taunted about his clubfoot (his own mother told him she had wanted to kill him at birth) and shortness (he finally reached five foot two). He was the sort who fought back with humor and, later, by wedding a string of beautiful women, including Tuesday Weld. A musical prodigy, Moore won a scholarship to Oxford and afterward teamed with longtime foil Peter Cook in mordant comedy sketches. He was in several films, notably *Bedazzled* (for which he wrote the score), *10* and *Arthur*, in which he delivered his best turn as a gleeful, wealthy dipsomaniac. He also played jazz piano on a number of albums. A rare brain disorder claimed him at 66.

Hulton Archive / Getty

Spike Milligan

Dudley Moore, Peter Cook, the Pythons and all other anarchic, postmodern British comedians owed an enormous debt to one Terence Milligan, patriarch of the Goons. In 1951 he teamed up with fellow ex-servicemen Peter Sellers, Harry Secombe and Michael Bentine to bring Milligan's idea for a surreal radio show to life on the BBC. Throughout the 1950s, the raucous skits and bits on *The Goon Show* kept Britain glued to the wireless, then the comedians went their separate ways. Milligan realized other successes as a writer and actor, but also great personal sadness as, having suffered shell shock during World War II, he battled bouts of deep depression until his death at age 83.

Michael Ochs Archives

Michael Abramson

Robert Urich

A critic got it right when he said, "If your mom never had a crush on Robert Urich, she didn't watch TV." For 25 years, he was never out of a regular series for more than three consecutive seasons, and he starred in a record 15 shows, from the early flop *Bob & Carol & Ted & Alice* to 2001's *bombe suprême,* the ephemeral *Emeril.* In between, his soulful, good-humored sexiness made him a tube heartthrob in a pair of tough-guy roles: as Dan Tanna in *Vega$* from 1978 through '81, then as the title character in *Spenser: For Hire* from 1985 through '88. The native Ohioan was only 55 when he died of cancer in California.

Linda Boreman

"I knew the feeling of a gun to my back and hearing the click," the New Yorker recalled in her memoirs, "never knowing when there was going to be a real bullet." Boreman said the man with the gun was first husband Chuck Traynor, forcing her into prostitution and pornography. In 1972, as Linda Lovelace, she starred in the landmark porn film *Deep Throat,* which made $600 million and, she said, paid her nothing. She escaped Traynor, remarried, had kids, survived a liver transplant and became a feminist and antiporn crusader. But a final tragedy awaited as Boreman, 53, died in Denver after a car crash.

Rosemary Clooney

When Rosemary (left) was young and lovely in the 1950s, so was her singing, whether in novelty items like "Come On-a My House," Irving Berlin ballads like those she shared with Bing Crosby in the film *White Christmas* or any number of other standards. By the 1980s and '90s—having survived stormy marriages and divorces, including two of each to Jose Ferrer; having beaten tranquilizers and sleeping pills; having recovered from a nervous breakdown; having gotten a wrecked career back on track—her voice was as deep as it was knowing, and more affecting than ever. Rosie was 74 when she died of lung cancer in Beverly Hills.

Bob Gomel

Peggy Lee

After a lousy childhood in North Dakota, where she was born Norma Deloris Egstrom in 1920, she began singing professionally at age 14. By 1941 she had signed with Benny Goodman's big band, and the next year she cut "Why Don't You Do Right?" Miss Peggy Lee (as she insisted on being introduced) was off on a long career served up in smoke, sizzle and a sultry swing whose flawless timing led Duke Ellington to dub her the Queen. When she sang "Lover," it gave folks "Fever." "Is That All There Is?" No, she also wrote many of her songs and was nominated for Best Supporting Actress for her role in 1955's *Pete Kelly's Blues*.

John Swoope

Dezo Hoffmann/Rex Features

Waylon Jennings

When the Texan died at 64 of a diabetes-related illness, he was eulogized for the wrong things. True, he was the member of Buddy Holly's Crickets who, in 1959, gave up his seat on the ill-fated plane. True, he was a pill-popping pal of young Johnny Cash. Yes, he was responsible for the *Dukes of Hazzard* theme. But the lonesome, on'ry and mean music that he and fellow Outlaws, including Willie Nelson, made in the 1960s and '70s was his real legacy. His Stratocaster blazing, Jennings reinvented country music.

John Entwistle

With his muscular hands, he hammered the bass like no other, earning the sobriquet Thunderfingers and providing the solid center of the storm that was the Who. When Roger Daltrey gave up guitar, Entwistle's moment arrived. He became one of rock's greatest bassists by blending rhythm and lead into a brand-new bottom. The Ox may have stood stock-still onstage, but his kinetic fingers set other bass players free. At age 57, he was found dead at the Hard Rock Hotel in Las Vegas, on the eve of a new Who tour.

Jean Catuffe/Sipa

Jay Mizell

Better known as the influential turntable pioneer Jam Master Jay, Mizell scratched and spun for the rap group Run-D.M.C. The 37-year-old New York City native was killed in a Queens studio in October with a bullet to the head. Married with three children, a campaigner against drug use, he was an unlikely victim in the turf wars that have plagued rap music. "Work for the good that Jay was working toward," said Darryl "D.M.C." McDaniel in his eulogy. "Peace for everybody."

Herman Leonard

Popsie Randolph/Frank Driggs Collection

Otis Blackwell

No one as important to the birth of rock 'n' roll was so little-known as this songwriter. Born in Brooklyn in 1931, he listened to black music, of course, but also loved country and western, which he heard at the movies; Tex Ritter always remained his favorite singer. Blackwell wrote or cowrote such classics as "Breathless," "Great Balls of Fire," "Handy Man," "Fever," and for Elvis, "Don't Be Cruel," "Paralyzed" and "All Shook Up." Because Presley couldn't read music, Blackwell sent tapes of his compositions, and may thereby have informed the King's style.

Lionel Hampton

As influential as he was flamboyant, the great jazz vibraphonist started out playing drums in a Chicago band made up of newsboys. His career was shaped by giants: Louis Armstrong urged the switch to vibes, and in 1936, Benny Goodman, having caught his act in L.A., invited him to join his group. Six years later, Hamp's own band recorded the soaring "Flying Home," whose fevered pace and ferocious rhythm has been cited as bedrock for rock 'n' roll. Hampton continued to teach and tour until shortly before his death in New York City at age 94.

Howell Conant

Michael Mauney

Bill Blass

Born to a Fort Wayne hardware salesman in 1922, he was smitten early on by elegant screen
beauties like Carole Lombard. After serving in Army counterintelligence during WWII, he worked his
way up the fashion tree and by the '60s he was at the top. Blass used touches from menswear to
bring sportswear couture to its pinnacle; his designs were subdued but never dull. Extremely well-
respected, he was able, it was once said, "to charm the clothes right onto a woman's back."

Ann Landers

"There will never be another Ann Landers," she once told *The New Yorker*. "When I go, the column goes with me." Esther (Eppie) Lederer assured this by purchasing the rights to her famous pseudonym. Her candid tone, which distinguished her advice column from most others, will be missed by her estimated 90 million readers (though surely some will seek counsel from "Dear Abby," the column founded by Esther's surviving twin, Pauline Esther Phillips, who suffers from Alzheimer's). In 1971, one of Landers's crusades influenced national affairs when President Richard M. Nixon signed the National Cancer Act, having received pressure from, among others, her army of readers. She herself died of cancer at age 83.

Yousuf Karsh

Born in Armenia in 1908, he escaped that war-torn land in 1924, emigrating with an uncle to Canada. A three-year apprenticeship with John Garo in Boston convinced Karsh that he should focus on the photographic portrait. A dramatic image of a seated, determined Churchill in 1941 brought Karsh renown, and in the years thereafter scores of leaders in the arts, sciences and politics peered into his lens. "My chief joy is to photograph the great in heart, in mind, and in spirit, whether they be famous or humble," Karsh once said. But many of his most famous portraits—Einstein, Hemingway, Picasso, Bardot, Bernstein, the Marx Brothers, Mother Teresa—are of the most famous people.

Sam Jones/Corbis Outline

The Toledo Blade

Chuck Jones

He was in on the creation of some of the world's greatest celebrities: Bugs Bunny, Daffy Duck, Porky Pig; by himself, he gave birth to Wile E. Coyote, the Road Runner and Pepe Le Pew. Born in Spokane in 1912, he and his family soon moved to Southern California, where Chuck, often cast as a child extra in movies, learned comic timing by observing Chaplin and Keaton. This, in tandem with his artistic flair, fueled more than 300 cartoons and led to Jones winning three Oscars. In collaboration with Dr. Seuss, he brought the Grinch to life on TV. When Jones died, a child asked, "Does this mean the bunny won't be in the barber chair anymore?" No, the bunny will be there forever.

Allan Grant

Mildred Benson

Nancy Drew, that teenage sleuth with the knack for narrowly escaping sticky situations, has attracted, over seven decades, a Harry Potter–esque number of readers. The person primarily responsible for drawing Drew's intrepid character was Benson, who, under the pseudonym Carolyn Keene, wrote 23 of the first 25 Nancy novels. She earned about $125 per book—plus Christmas bonuses—and had to sign away not only royalties but also any attempts at personal recognition. Benson, who was also a journalist, went to her *Toledo Blade* office regularly until her death at 96.

Ruth Handler

The male executives at Mattel were resistant to the concept of a curvy, adultlike doll, but designer Ruth Handler persisted, and in 1959, Barbie was ready for her coming out. A little more than four decades later, more than a billion Barbies have been sold. This doesn't please everyone. In the 1970s feminists began to criticize the doll's preposterous proportions and the whole Barbie message. Mattel adapted, issuing working-woman versions—each one still an absolute doll. Through her plastic friend, said Handler, who died at 85, a "little girl could be anything she wanted to be."

Stephen Jay Gould

America's foremost essayist on natural science, the quirky, crusty Harvard evolutionary biologist made complex matters not only accessible but irresistible to readers. His topics took flight from his creative points of demarcation, such as Mickey Mouse or his beloved baseball. Gould's influence, however, transcended the lay audience. He was a powerful figure in paleontology and related fields; typically, that sort of fame attracted critics as well as disciples. In any event, he was, in all likelihood, the best-known biologist since Darwin. Gould succumbed to cancer at age 60.

Owen/Black Star

Wally McNamee/Woodfin Camp & Assoc.

W. Eugene Smith

Stephen E. Ambrose

He wasn't a great analytical historian, nor was he a dazzling stylist, but he was a gifted bookmaker, able to weave narrative and personal recollections into accounts that were entertaining and often intensely moving. As a boy during WWII, Ambrose (below) considered returning vets "giants who had saved the world," and his focus became men in crisis—Nixon, Ike and, most memorably, "ordinary" soldiers, whose bravery he celebrated, fueling the way for a renewed appreciation for those who fought in that war. Regrettably, not long before he fell victim to lung cancer at age 66, his career was tainted by charges of plagiarism.

Walter Annenberg

In 1940 the 32-year-old college dropout inherited the family business when his father, Moses (above), an immigrant who made a fortune with the *Daily Racing Form* and then *The Philadelphia Inquirer,* was jailed for tax evasion. To everyone's astonishment, the insecure scion whose nickname was "Boy" succeeded wildly. In 1944 he launched *Seventeen,* a huge hit, and a decade later *TV Guide,* which at its peak sold nearly 20 million copies a week. Walter Annenberg, who died at 94, served as Nixon's ambassador to Great Britain, assembled a stellar art collection and gave away more than $1 billion—some said to cleanse the family name.

Moira B. Ambrose

Thor Heyerdahl

To adventurers, Heyerdahl, who died at 87, was a renowned anthropologist. To many anthropologists, he was an adventurous amateur. To the wider world, the Norwegian was a visionary Viking with a poet's soul, a man to whom nothing was impossible. His 1970 voyage on the primitive *Ra II* may (or may not) have proved that ancient Egyptians, crossing the Atlantic from Morocco to the West Indies, beat Columbus to the New World. His most famous float, the 101-day *Kon-Tiki* epic from South America to Polynesia in 1947, may (or may not) have rewritten theories of Pacific migration. But they proved beyond doubt that when Heyerdahl set out to do a thing, the thing got done.

JUST ONE MORE

It was a day just like 364 others on the Staten Island Ferry in New York Harbor, and yet it was not at all like the rest. It was September 11, 2002, and everyone aboard was aware that precisely one year ago the Manhattan skyline had forever been altered by terrorism. If the resonance of that infamous date was more acute on the anniversary, it nevertheless was felt throughout the world all year long.

Photograph by Rob Ostermaier